Dawna,

A special classmate & friend

Blessings,

Dave Pinto

Lorraine M. Pinto

7/29/12

KIDS DON'T BUILD BOATS

David E. Plante *with* Lorraine M. Plante

CROSSBOOKS
PUBLISHING

CrossBooks™
A Division of LifeWay
1663 Liberty Drive
Bloomington, IN 47403
www.crossbooks.com
Phone: 1-866-879-0502

First published by CrossBooks 06/28/2011

ISBN: 978-1-6150-7908-7 (sc)
ISBN: 978-1-6150-7910-0 (hc)

Library of Congress Control Number: 2011931189

Printed in the United States of America

This book is printed on acid-free paper.

Captain of his dream

Lorraine and I dedicate this book to

Sharon and Greg,
our daughter and son-in-law.

Sharon, you love your freedom, your horses, and
the wide, open space of Texas country.

Greg, as a major in the US Army, you serve and protect
the freedoms of our country—we honor you.

Acknowledgments

A special thanks to my longtime friend, Richard Johnson. After sharing many of my stories with you, you encouraged me and suggested that I write them down in a book. Without your encouragement, Richard, this book never would have been born.

And, of course, many deserved thanks to all those at CrossBooks who shared their expertise and made the publication of our first book a reality.

Contents

Introduction

Life in New England during and immediately following World War II was difficult. The challenge of living day-to-day with what was available and squeezing happiness out of close relationships was critical to survival.

Jacob was an independent, strong-willed, and by his own admission, troubled child. He was born to be free from control. Jacob's relationship with his mom and grandparents significantly influenced his childhood but had little impact on his desire for freedom. That desire, however, was enhanced by his father's absence in the evenings. Jacob's desire for freedom, pitted against the then accepted method of physical discipline he faced, created a unique childhood experience with significant risks and rewards.

This true story is as much about the environment Jacob lived in and the individuals who loved him, as it is about the problems he created and the challenges he faced. Each one tried to help him mature, compete successfully, and grow into normalcy, in spite of him being a thief and believing he contributed to the death of a neighbor. His guilt consumed him. Only when his self-image was at its lowest point did the solution become self-evident.

This story was documented not only to share the adventures as well as the trials and tribulations of Jacob's fretful youth, but so that others finding themselves in Jacob's position or with a child like Jacob, will realize that there is a reason for hope; and it is within their grasp.

The individual and corporate names have sometimes been changed to protect their privacy and to avoid suggesting that any one of them was responsible for Jacob's fumbles.

CHAPTER 1

Protectors

In the mid-1940s, while our country was engaged in World War II, my dad was serving overseas in the army. During his service time, my mother, my one-year-older sister, Julie, and I, Jacob, were blessed to be able to live with my maternal grandparents in my hometown of Rochester, New Hampshire.

We slept upstairs in a large bedroom on the back side of the house. The room contained twin junior-sized beds. Mom and Julie slept in one bed, and I—then three but anxious to be four years old—slept in the other. The bedroom had been added to the house by my grandfather to accommodate his third and fourth children, my mom and my Aunt Beverly.

My grandparents' home faced a huge lumberyard with elevated train tracks running past it. Grandpa worked as a boiler engineer at the lumberyard. His job was to keep the boilers and related equipment running, thereby providing electricity for the plant and the offices. The power plant burned wood trimmings, so the boiler needed frequent cleaning, which was also his responsibility. Grandpa, six feet four inches tall with long arms and weighing over two hundred twenty pounds, would crawl into it, clean it, and replace damaged bricks when necessary. He never complained about his work. To me, he was a giant, towering over everything around him.

The early morning winter sun was especially beautiful as it rose and peeked through the low-lying clouds shortly after the train blew its whistle at seven o'clock. When I heard the whistle, which sounded louder in the winter than any other time of the year, I jumped out of bed, ran to the bedroom window, and daydreamed as I watched the lengthy train roll noisily down the tracks, headed for places unknown to me. How I wished I were old enough to hitch a ride.

I loved watching the train as it passed by. It was like seeing a moving picture postcard. For the longest time, the smoke from the engine floated above the passing train. The snow-covered ground resembled a frozen ocean and the stacks of lumber, Chinese junks. What a way to start a day!

It was a project for me just to get ready to spend a winter morning outside. It took me longer to get my outer clothes and boots on than it took me to eat my breakfast. By the time I finished dressing and putting on my mittens, I was hot and could barely move. I had to get outside in a hurry to cool off.

Three doors stood between me and the outside. The kitchen door opened to the woodshed, the woodshed door opened to the back porch, and the back porch door opened to the rear steps. The multiple doors kept the kitchen warm and almost draft free. Once outside, I felt as if I had just left Noah's ark.

—⟊—

I loved the snow. We got 60 to140 inches of it during the winter and snow would eventually be piled high along the driveway and walkway out to the garage and the chicken house. The huge snowbanks were perfect for building forts.

One day, I decided to build my fort at the end of the driveway where the city snowplow and those who'd shoveled the driveway had piled the snow the highest. I carved steps into the walls of snow and ice along the driveway so that I could climb up and build my snow fort.

The fort was easy to dig out of the top of the snowbank. I used the shovel the adults used to take ashes out of the bottom of the wood-burning kitchen stove. (In winter, that shovel and a bucket of ashes were kept near the rear steps so that anyone could spread ashes on the slippery ice.) After I cut individual blocks of snow, I made a wall around the fort, leaving spaces between the blocks to look through. With the fort completed, I turned my attention to making a stack of snowballs and waited, ready for action.

No one was around, so I waited and waited. I figured some neighborhood kids would eventually come out to play. One car went by; then it was quiet for a long time. When it's quiet in the winter, it's really quiet. It was midmorning when I heard the sound of another car coming slowly down the street. I stayed crouched down and hidden behind the wall but decided it couldn't hurt to toss a couple of snowballs toward the car. I'd probably miss anyway, wrapped up as I was in winter clothing.

As the car approached, I grabbed a snowball and tossed it haphazardly over the wall in the direction of the car. I grabbed another, stood up, and threw it as hard as I could. I don't know where the first snowball landed, but the second one went into the open car window and hit the driver on his left cheek.

He abruptly stopped his car, got out, and headed toward the driveway. Knowing I was in big trouble, I slid down the banking and into the driveway. Hoping to make a quick escape before this angry man caught me, I started running as fast as my snowsuit would allow. Just then, I noticed that the back porch door was open and Grammy was hastily coming down the steps. I thought to myself, *If one doesn't get me, the other one will.* Fearing what the stranger had in mind to do to me more than Grammy's punishment, I quickly headed toward her.

Grammy was a short woman, but she got between me and the rosy-cheeked, angry man who was furiously declaring that I needed a good beating. Her hands moving while she defended me, Grammy acknowledged that I had made a mistake and would be punished, but she also made it clear that it would not be by him. The stranger finally backed off and slowly headed back down the driveway, all the while mumbling about what he would like to do to me.

Grammy took my hand and led me up the stairs, into the back porch, and to the woodshed where she instructed me to take off my snowsuit and boots because she didn't want me to get the kitchen floor wet.

"I've made some muffins," she said. "We'll have tea, milk, and a midmorning snack together."

Her cheeks were red, and her long, normally braided hair hung loosely over her face. She looked younger and more alive than I had ever seen her before. I knew I would love her forever, and I believe she knew I would never throw snowballs at moving cars again.

As Grammy drank her tea, she giggled as she repeated some of the words the man had said to us just a few minutes earlier. It was great to watch and hear her laugh. I was overcome with her courage and her patience with me.

—*m*—

While summers at my grandparents' home were filled with working in the gardens, feeding the chickens, and cleaning their pens, there was always time for fun. Some Saturdays when it was really hot, Grandpa drove us to the Isinglass River in Barrington, a small town about seven miles southwest of Rochester. The roads to Barrington were tarred for the first four miles and dirt the remainder of the way to the river. The river flowed east to meet the Cocheco River below Rochester. (The name *Isinglass* refers to the shiny mica sometimes found on the river bottom.)

When we went to the river, we usually went as a family and took a picnic lunch. Uncles, aunts, and cousins came along, and we made a day of it. The river wasn't large, but it flowed quite fast over some large boulders. Pools of water below the boulders were like small ponds. Some were seven or eight feet deep. All the adults knew how to swim, but I hadn't yet learned. When the adults ran and jumped off the boulders into the water, I could only watch.

I told Grandpa I wanted to learn how to swim, so he said, "Come on," and led me into the deeper part of the river. I heard my mother hollering something from the bank but couldn't understand what she was saying. I turned and got a glimpse of her waving her hands as I fell off Grandpa's shoulders and into the cold water.

I was about a foot under water; it was so clear that I could see Grandpa's long arms pushing me away from him as I tried to reach out for him. I wasn't scared, just ignorant of what I was supposed to do. I started swallowing water, yet somehow came to the surface.

He said, "Paddle!" as he picked me up and dropped me back into the water.

We went through this routine three or four times until I began to get annoyed. Was I the dumbest kid in the world or was he playing games with me? How many times did I see his tall body moving away from me as I struggled under the water? I'd come to the surface, look around, and back underwater I'd go. I stopped, caught my breath, and thought to myself, *This isn't right.* I hit the water again, but this time I headed away from him and paddled my arms as fast as I could.

I heard him yell out, "You got it!"

To me, I hadn't gotten anything except too many mouthfuls of water and a new distrust for this really tall giant. I looked up to see my mother (who was still in her dress) waist deep in the water on her way to rescue me. Someone was laughing, but it wasn't us.

We both recovered, and—you know the rest of the story. I had learned to swim, thanks to Grandpa. Even though Mom knew Grandpa would never have let me drown, her rescue confirmed to everyone at the river that I was still her pet and spoiled rotten.

—⚏—

My grandparents' kitchen always smelled delightful. I couldn't pass by the new refrigerator without opening it. On the top shelf was a small dish with three prunes in it. There was always some vanilla ice cream in the small freezer. Grammy told me I could eat anything in the pantry, refrigerator, or freezer, except for her three prunes and Grandpa's ice cream. I understood the importance of ice cream but had no idea why she ate three prunes every morning.

—⚏—

Although I loved living with them, I'll never forget the day that Dad returned from overseas. He came in on a late train, so Julie and I went to sleep. When we awoke, he was there in our bedroom. We were ecstatic! It was a wonderful family reunion with lots of hugs, laughter, and tears of joy, for we were finally together again.

Jacob sitting atop his fort

CHAPTER 2

Long Turns in the Autumn

Many people today don't own cars, which surprises some folks. In the mid-1940s, however, not having a car was normal. As a young child, I thought living with my grandparents was great for many reasons, including the fact that they owned a car and we didn't.

As I've already said, Grandpa was a tall man with very long arms. When he drove, he never touched the top of the steering wheel. He turned the steering wheel by sliding the bottom of it through both hands. This was a slow process, so most of his turns were long, sweeping events. He wasn't a fast driver, which was both good and bad. Good because you had time to see cars coming and avoid them, and bad because each turn seemed to take forever. This was okay in the country on wide roads but not on sharp curves or in the city on narrow streets with tight corners.

Every year at fall foliage time, we'd spend a whole day in the majestic White Mountains. The best part of the trip was touring the mountains and seeing all the hardwood trees adorned with their brilliant fall colors. Usually, several cars loaded with uncles, aunts, and cousins went along. My family always rode with my grandparents. Grandpa drove, and on every sharp curve the girls screamed until he was back on our side of the road. I believed the screaming encouraged him and sometimes made my dad smile.

I preferred to ride in the backseat with Mom. I not only saw better from there but could also watch Dad sitting in the front hugging the passenger door. Even though his face turned white as we went around some of the curves on the mountain roads, he kept his thoughts to himself.

Fall foliage day was usually a success. But I never really knew if we were going to get home alive. In fact, I thought what Grandpa did was dangerous and for his own entertainment.

Grandpa liked to tease, and I wondered if his teasing was the same as that referred to in the Scripture: "And, ye fathers provoke not your children to wrath: but bring them up in the nurture and admonition of the Lord" (Ephesians 6:4). It wasn't my place to judge him or anyone else, but perhaps fewer long turns on these trips might have brought him and my dad closer together. But who knows?

After arriving home from a full day in the mountains with Grandpa in the driver's seat, I finally relaxed—the pressure was off. Everyone met at Grammy's for the evening meal, which we called *supper*. Grammy and the aunts had planned it out to the last detail the week before.

The meal always included plenty of hot vegetables, at least two types of protein with one usually being chicken, salads, hot rolls with butter, hot coffee, tea, and plain and chocolate milk for the kids. Dessert was an avalanche of homemade pies, cakes, and cookies, with each family bringing their best to share. Eating as a family was important to us and contentiousness was not even imagined. Eating together took time; no one hurried.

The cleanup process was just as much fun as supper. The men and children headed for other rooms in the house while the women did their part like a well-organized operating-room team, including the appropriate discussion of critical current events.

Post-supper naps were timely. My grandparents took the lead in their favorite living room chairs with some of the uncles and aunts following suit. Grandpa's favorite chair faced the front porch window. Normally, it was a familiar sight to see him sitting there with a newspaper in hand. After he finished a section of it, he'd drop it to the floor next to his chair. It was a big deal to grab the sections Grandpa had dropped and then sit on the living room floor and read them.

The papers reported that last year over 2 million returning veterans had attended colleges and universities on the G.I. Bill of Rights, and they estimated that this year 50 percent of all college tuitions would be paid for by the government. I hoped my dad would think about finishing school.

President Truman was always in the news. During the summer, he had given a speech declaring forcefully that the Constitution guarantees equal rights for blacks. He also signed a bill approved by Congress introducing the Marshall Plan that would spend over 13 billion dollars to help Europe recover from World War II.

As young as I was, I couldn't see enough pictures about the rest of the world. Living in a small town was great, but in my heart I knew there was a lot more to life and I hoped to someday see some of it firsthand.

At around eight o'clock, someone got the games out and the evening of laughter and moderate teasing began. Dad wasn't a great game player, so he and one of my uncles sat on the back stairs sharing smokes and a few stories. With the next day being Sunday, there was no pressure to head home early. Sunday school and church didn't start until nine-thirty, so most of us could sleep in.

Grandpa and Grammy—hearts of gold

CHAPTER 3

Night Rail Riding

Shortly after my dad came home from serving in the South Pacific, we moved into our own home on Franklin Street, about a half mile from my grandparents' home.

Our one-story home, with two acres of good top soil property, sat on the top of a small hill. The house had an open front porch the width of the house, with a neat four-foot wall enclosing it. The sides of the front steps were also enclosed. Two sugar maple trees on the front lawn shaded the house.

The front door opened into the living room, which had a fireplace. Across from the living room, on the front side of the house, was Julie's bedroom. As you walked through the living room towards the back of the house, French doors separated it from the dining room. The dining room had side bay windows that faced the driveway and the neighboring field.

On the other side of the dining room, at the back side of the house, was the kitchen. It had wooden floors, an ice box, and a stove that burned both wood and kerosene. The kitchen changed gradually over the first couple of years, with the purchase of a refrigerator and electric stove. Later, a cement pad was poured in the dirt basement for a cold-storage area and a new freezer.

Our one bathroom was off a short hallway next to the kitchen. It contained a cast-iron, claw-foot bathtub; a sink; and a toilet under the window. Along the wall next to the sink and on the way to the toilet, was

11

a small, white hamper for dirty clothes. Two more bedrooms, my parents' and mine, were across from each other at the far end of the hallway.

The boiler in the basement burned wood and coal, and it provided plenty of steam radiator heat during the winter. There was no air conditioning, so when the weather was warm, the windows were open much of the time, particularly on the shady side of the house. On the sunny side, the pull-down window shades helped to keep the house cool. The three-bedroom house was comfortable and the perfect size for us.

—ᴡ—

Although I'd left my grandparents' home physically, I guess I was still mentally there at night. I dreamed about waking up in the morning to the sound of the train's whistle and running to the window and watching the train head down the track at seven o'clock. Somehow, my dreams included a new bike and my attempts to ride that bike on the steel tracks while trying to catch up to the moving train.

Night after night, I had the same dream about riding my new bike on the steel train tracks. In the early part of my dream, I balanced the bike on the single rail just fine. I pumped hard and headed down the track without a worry.

As the dream progressed, however, the two parallel tracks got smaller and closer together. It became harder to balance the bike on the single rail. The sky around me blackened, and I was about to head into a dark, deep tunnel and couldn't slow down. My arms began to tire, my legs became heavy, and I knew I couldn't lift them to get off the bike before it crashed somewhere in the bowels of the tunnel.

Headed for big trouble, I tried to scream but couldn't. My lips wouldn't move. I tried to roll off the speeding bike by swinging my body back and forth. At this point, I woke up only to find that I'd wet my bed. I was so embarrassed and upset. This was terrible! I thought over and over again, *I've got to find some way to stop dreaming this stupid dream.*

The next time I started dreaming about riding the bike down the train tracks, I tried to think fast but couldn't. I thought to myself, *I have to end this ride before the bike gets moving too fast for me to get off.* I was heading down the track and picking up speed. I had to jump off, but I couldn't move my arms and my legs felt heavy again. This time I got mad, really mad, and intentionally drove the bike off the tracks and into the darkness.

I was elated when I woke up and found I hadn't wet my bed, but I had to quickly head for the bathroom. I had finally solved my problem. Thereafter, every time I caught myself in that dream, I'd get mad and ride my bike off the track and into the darkness.

Around that same period of time, the family was talking about an unusual smell in the bathroom. Some days it was there and some days it wasn't. It seemed to come from the white wicker hamper with the imitation dark marbled lid.

I didn't think much about the smell in the hamper until one night when I had the same old dream. I jumped off the bike in my dream and, once awake, climbed out of bed and headed to the bathroom. I lifted the lid of the toilet and began my duty. Opening my eyes further, I realized I was peeing in the hamper. I was shocked and moved quickly to the toilet. How could I be doing this?

When I went back to bed, I couldn't sleep. Now there was another problem to solve. I needed help but couldn't tell anyone about my problem. I tried to figure out a way to make sure that when I got out of bed, I'd make myself really wake up. How could I do that? Now, when the conversation in the house turned to the unusual smell in the hamper, I just kept my eyes lowered and said nothing.

The next time I had that dream, I climbed out of bed and headed into the bathroom. I didn't know it, but help was on the way. Shortly after dropping my pajama bottoms and lifting the lid, I felt a familiar sharp pain in my right butt when Dad spanked me. I was immediately wide awake. My hand was clinging to the hamper lid.

My dad asked, "What are you doing?"

"I don't know, Dad. I really don't know what I'm doing."

Dad was bent down and appeared ready to take a second shot, so I dropped the lid and pulled up my pajamas. I didn't have to go to the bathroom anymore. Without looking up, I tried to quickly walk around him. That didn't work, but all he said was, "Don't do it again!"

"I'll try not to," was all I could think to reply.

The smell in the bathroom improved. No one said anything about the night Dad found me in there. I still had the bike-and-train dreams, but I had learned how to crash quickly and roll out of bed as I was waking up.

I'm sure that many people today would disagree with the quick, sharp lesson he taught me, but I'm glad he did it. I was in serious trouble and needed a wake-up call.

I continued to have wonderful dreams and almost no nightmares. When I reflected on why I stopped at the hamper, I concluded that it was my first target of opportunity, and I didn't have to bend down to flip the cover open. Therefore, speed and convenience were the primary drivers.

Home

CHAPTER 4

Mom's Loving Friend

I was standing on the kitchen counter looking down at the floor. How had I gotten here? What had I said or done to have to experience this? Mom and Mom's loving friend were laughing, but to me there was nothing funny.

They had put a dress on me and that made me fighting mad. I was no pervert, and girls' clothes looked great on them but not on me. The dress had no color, or I was too upset to remember anything except the white collar and white fringe on the short sleeves. I kicked as hard as I could and was able to prevent them from putting girls' socks on me. As I looked at Mom's friend, I thought, *Why do bad things happen to me when you are around?*

Mom's friend said, "When you act like a girl, you will be dressed like a girl."

How had I acted like a girl? I had no idea.

Grandpa, in my opinion, was a wise man. He had a saying: One boy is a man, two boys are half a man, and three boys are no man at all. Up until that day, I had wondered if it also applied to women. It was no longer an unanswered question. When my mom's friend was around, Mom turned into a girl and was no longer the mature mom I relied on.

During the Second World War, Uncle Ted, my mother's older brother, served in the Army Post Office on an island off the coast of Maine. My mother; her friend; my sister, Julie; and I went to visit him on the island. The boat ride to the island was fun until my mother took Julie to the rest room. Mom's friend was to keep her eye on me.

The boat was quite large with wood-covered steel railings all the way around both the upper and lower decks. We were standing on the lower deck under the steel stairs, leaning on a white storage container. There were very few people on the boat, and we were the only ones on that side.

I remarked to Mom's friend that I couldn't see very well. She lifted me up and stood me on the storage box—the one we had been leaning on. "Can you see now?" she asked.

I replied, "Not that well because of the stairs."

She picked me up and hung me over the railing. "Can you see now?"

I couldn't speak. I was terrified! Finally, she pulled me back behind the railing and stood me on the box again. I thought to myself, *This woman is nuts!* What was she thinking? Why hang me out over the water?

When my mom and sister returned, I told Mom what had happened. She laughed. "You have such an imagination, Jacob!"

That was true, but Mom's friend was taking advantage of my mother's trust. I knew I had to avoid baiting her or doing anything that would upset her, or it was over the side for me.

—⁂—

Sometimes, when Mom needed to run errands, Mom's friend babysat us. I tried to stay out of her way by playing outdoors. Julie would come out and play for a while, get dirty, and then go back inside. On one particular day while she was babysitting us, we were both outside playing when she called us to come in and get cleaned up for lunch.

"You two are really dirty. Get your clothes off and jump into the tub."

She ran the water and Julie got into the tub. I wouldn't get in until she'd finished filling it. I had learned not to trust Mom's friend.

She handed us each a bar of soap and said, "Scrub." She watched and then remarked, "You aren't getting all the dirt off." She left the room and came back with a gallon container of Clorox bleach, and then she poured some into the water. It smelled so strong. She mixed it into the bathwater and again told us to "Scrub."

We heard the back screen door slam shut. Mom was home from her errands. I heard her put the groceries away. As she walked into the bathroom she asked, "What is that smell?" Mom's friend told her.

Mom carefully washed and rinsed us with fresh water as if we were smelly fish. Her friend left the room after Mom's pointed comments about what "never" to do to us again.

My skin didn't burn much, but I had some red spots. However, Julie's skin was irritated and sore for a few days. We had both survived, but I often wondered what the chances of survival would have been if she had babysat us for a whole weekend. For the next couple of weeks, Mom's friend and my mom weren't as close as usual—which was normally like glue.

—⚏—

One day, the four of us visited my grandparents' house in the middle of the day. We climbed the stairs to the back porch door, and Mom went inside. We waited as she unlocked the house door, and then my sister and Mom's friend quickly followed her into the house. Before I could enter, however, someone closed and locked the house door from the inside. I was out on the porch alone. I looked through one of the two porch windows into the kitchen. They were nowhere to be seen. They had left the kitchen and headed for some other part of the house.

I could have sat down and relaxed and waited for them to return. I could have gone back outside and climbed a tree or had some fun. No, not me; I got upset and banged on the door. No one came. I tried again, but still no one even came to the window. I stood outside the window and waited. Julie showed up first, then Mom's friend, and then Mom came to the large window. They stood there waving, smiling, and making a big deal of being inside while I was outside.

Why I did it, I don't know, but I smashed the window hard with my right fist, and it crashed into the kitchen. I fell on the windowsill but didn't go through the window. My hand was cut, but it wasn't serious—breaking the window *was* serious.

They quickly bandaged my hand. There was a lot of conversation, but no one had the answer as to what to do about the broken window. They swept up the pieces of shattered glass as Mom continued to say under her breath, "I can't believe you smashed the window; I can't believe you smashed the window!"

Mom hooked the latch on the storm door of the enclosed porch to prevent anyone from climbing into the house through the broken window. She locked the back door, and we all left the house through the front door. We then headed to Grammy's workplace to tell her about the window and to see if she had any ideas on how to replace it quickly.

By the time Grandpa got home, we were all in the kitchen looking forward to supper, but not looking forward to his questions about the broken window. He asked very little and then proceeded through the kitchen to the porch and out to the back workshop. I followed and watched him pull down a storm window from the rack and head back to the house. He hung the storm window on its hooks above the empty window frame and went into the house. He then pulled the storm window closed and tightly screwed the clips on each side of the window.

"There, that will hold us for a while," he remarked. Then he washed his hands and was ready for supper. My kind of guy! Rights the sinking ship quickly, washes his hands, and is ready for chow!

—⁂—

In a large family, you have many reasons to celebrate. In my opinion, there was no better place than at Grandpa's house to do that. This day of celebration had something to do with Mom's friend. We were all in the kitchen, and she was sitting in my grandfather's chair telling a story. I was sitting on the floor a few feet away, listening.

Mom's friend was like Grandpa in many ways. She was smart and verbally quick, and she loved to tease and play practical jokes. She was very social—if the room was too quiet, she'd start the conversation (she could talk to anyone about anything). Like Grandpa, she was also a very hard worker. She loved music and could pick up any musical instrument and within a short while was able to play a tune on it. But most important to many of her friends and relatives was the fact that she had the wisdom to marry a very nice guy.

In the middle of telling her story, she stopped, looked at me, and accused me of looking up her dress. She then went on with her story, but I got that perverted look from the rest of the family. In response, I said as loudly and convincingly as I could, "I was not looking up your dress!"

I wanted to throw her through the window. I didn't like losing it, but around Mom's friend I was running on ice, ready to crash at any minute. I needed to find something else to do, far away from her.

Elsa, my oldest cousin, came up to me and asked, "Why were you looking up her dress?"

I tried to convince her that I wasn't, but I was wasting my time. It appeared to me that once charged by one woman with a sex crime, you are guilty until proven innocent by another woman.

Elsa then asked, "What are you going to do now?"

"Go out and play."

"But it's raining," she said.

I then asked her, "Do you know how to walk on stilts?"

She responded, "No, what are they?"

I explained that they were two tall poles with a block nailed to each one about two feet off the ground. You placed your feet on the blocks, which elevated you. Then, you walked like you were six feet tall.

We headed out to the shed to see if we could find some two-by-twos, blocks, hammers, and nails. We were in luck. Grandpa's garage was half garage and half workshop. We found everything we needed and proceeded to make the stilts.

Even though it was raining, we stayed outside and walked on the stilts until Elsa's mother told her to come in out of the rain. We headed down the bulkhead steps and into the basement. Using the basement wall to lean against, we climbed onto the stilts. Then we walked all around the basement. Elsa and I laughed when either one of us crashed.

Elsa said, "I bet you can't walk down the basement stairs on stilts."

"How much will you bet me?"

She had a buck and that was enough for me. She stayed at the bottom near the water meter, which was in front of the bottom step. I headed up the stairs and quietly opened the door. No one was in the den, so I set my stilts against the door frame and stepped up on them. The ceiling above the stairs was very close to my head, so I proceeded slowly. It started out okay because there was a wall on both sides of the stairs that I could lean on. Each step was followed with a bump against the wall. I straightened up and then took the next step down.

I knew Elsa well enough to know that in order to earn the buck I had to walk down all of the steps, so I took my time. When halfway down the stairs, I stopped and realized that on one side I could see out the basement window and on the other side, clear through the basement. It was great to be six feet tall, just like Grandpa.

Enjoying the view, I lost focus and missed my next step—leaving the stilts and heading south. I hit the wall and the ground about the same time Elsa screamed. Only God knows what they were thinking upstairs. Before we knew it, the stairs were filled with adults.

I heard my mother ask, "Are you awake, Jacob? Can you hear me?"

"Yes, but my head and knee hurt."

I also heard a comment like: "That was a dumb thing to try to do." I recognized the voice. Mom's loving friend was close by.

We all went upstairs and after some Band-Aids and a glass of milk, all was well but not forgotten. I looked for Elsa and hoped to talk her out of the buck I felt I'd earned.

CHAPTER 5

Wake-Up Calls

When I was about five years old, Mom and I went shopping at our local F. W. Woolworth five-and-ten-cent store. We almost never went downtown shopping together, but she had borrowed Grammy's car and this time had taken me along.

She was focused on items on the shelves; I was roaming but not too far away from her. All of a sudden, she slapped each of my hands. Broken pieces of cookies dropped to the store floor. *What had I done*, I wondered?

She sternly said, "Come with me," and walked me to the store manager's office. During the walk to the office, I realized I'd been stealing cookies out of the cookie bins along the wall and eating them as though they were samples.

"Jacob, tell him what you did and why."

I told him what I knew about what I had done, but that wasn't much. I didn't know why I had done it, so my response was short. Mom gave me a dollar to pay the manager. I told him I was sorry and gave him the money. He appeared surprised by the visit, but he played the role Mom wanted him to play, and he thanked her.

Once outside the store, Mom didn't say much but had a firm grasp of my hand as we walked quickly to the car. In reflection, I believe she was still in shock and very surprised by what I had done. I surprised her many times in my life, but what she may not have realized was that most of those times I surprised myself as well.

They say that timing is everything, and my mom's timing was perfect. I needed someone to tell me where I was, what I had done wrong, and make me never forget it. I obviously also needed to learn more respect for other people's property. I concluded this wasn't a habit I had picked up. Because cavalierly eating everything in sight at home came so natural to me, it may have been I just needed a wake-up call.

I didn't really mind that she had involved the store manager to make a point, but I just hoped I hadn't lost her as a friend. Up until that day she had been my mother, protector, and friend. From that day forward, however, I wasn't sure about the friend part. Therefore, I set my mind to earning back her respect and friendship.

I was a daydreamer and wasn't sure how I was going to change. Daydreaming really bothered me. Night dreaming was great most of the time, but daydreaming made me feel slightly out of control, and that feeling was uncomfortable. I knew it had something to do with my lack of focusing on the present, staying busy, and being productive. There was plenty of work to do around the house. So after deciding that I wanted a piece of the action, I kept busy doing a number of the chores.

Even though weeding the garden wasn't my favorite task, I accepted it as my responsibility and enjoyed the feeling of accomplishment as I finished weeding each row. I kept my bedroom neat and my toys out of sight when they weren't in use. I volunteered to feed the chickens twice a day. My parents agreed. After a testing period, they stopped asking me twice a day if the chickens had been fed and watered. I jumped at the chance to shovel snow whenever it was needed. The shovels were large, but I was gaining strength. The path to the chicken house, which I felt was part of my territory, had to be cleared first. After that I helped clear the driveway, which was wide and long.

I learned to enjoy finishing tasks. Each task I finished made me feel like a functioning part of the family. I realized that lying around the house was just another opportunity to daydream, to irritate Julie, to upset Mom, and to unconsciously do something stupid.

My mom's respect and friendship were important to me. I enjoyed thinking of her as my best friend. I knew that the day we spent shopping in the five-and-ten-cent store was my first wake-up call, and I also knew that I'd never take her respect and friendship for granted again.

I learned very young that good friends are hard to find. A fellow Sunday school classmate lived on Portland Street, not far away. I sometimes walked to his place, and we just horsed around. Other times, he came to my house. We swapped stories and climbed trees in the woods behind my home.

One day, Mom told me he had contracted lockjaw. She said that it is a serious bacterial disease that usually comes from animal manure. It starts with stiffness in the jaw and neck and can move throughout the body. She assured me that he, being young and strong, would recover in time, but unfortunately many of the elderly die of it each year.

I couldn't visit him because I might catch it; so I called him on the phone and left many messages saying that I missed my friend and hoped he would get well soon. With my mom's help, I sent several get-well cards to him. I not only missed him but also worried about him. Mom told me that sending cards and calling was the right thing to do and not to worry about the fact that he hadn't responded. I remembered he had lockjaw, so how was my sick friend able to respond?

My friend didn't attend Sunday school for months. When he did recover, he came back to Sunday school and just said, "Hello." That was it! No thank you for the cards and no comment about the left messages. After that experience, I decided that there are acquaintances and friends. One difference between the two is that friends return left messages and thank you for the cards and concern.

Dan Morton's dad owned a bike shop near the grammar school that Julie and I attended. Dan and I became friends in school and spent time playing together after school. He lived on the other side of the railroad tracks and lumberyard across from my grandparents' house.

We spent hours climbing the lumber piles near the railroad tracks and building forts with the lumber trimmings. The lumber hadn't dried out yet, so it was green and very flexible. The stacked lumber was separated by trimmings so that air could pass through each layer of planks or boards. Some of the longer boards stuck out of the stack four to six feet above the ground and resembled diving boards ready for use.

We played a game, the object of which was to walk out to the end of the board and jump as high as you could without breaking the board. Dan was not only larger and stronger than I, but also much more aggressive. I watched him jump higher and higher until I thought for sure the board would break and he'd get hurt.

He was the first friend I had who took more risk than I did. It sincerely bothered me but not for competitive reasons—I was concerned for his safety. He didn't break the board; nevertheless, I thought he had pushed it too far and told him so.

Later in the week, we were again climbing stacks of lumber when we noticed a freight train slowly coming down the track. He hollered, "Watch this!" Then he ran out on the track way ahead of the train and stood with his arms crossed. The train engineer blew the whistle as the train gained speed. Dan just stood there. The engineer blew it again and again, and Dan still stood there defiantly with his arms crossed. The train was really moving now. I started screaming at him to jump, but the whistle was louder than my screams. Then Dan was gone.

I was already off the stacked lumber and running parallel to the passing train. The train was pulling away from me as I looked under the freight cars hoping to see him standing on the other side of the tracks, but he wasn't there. All I could think was that he must be stuck to the front of the train. Suddenly, he jumped up from the other side of the tracks. He had jumped off the train tracks and into a five-foot-deep hollow a few yards away from the tracks. I was relieved to see him standing there, but I was ticked.

I asked myself, *What is wrong with my friend?* Just a week before, I had encouraged him not to jump so hard on a diving board, and today he put his life in danger and tested the patience of a train engineer by standing in front of the train. Did he have a death wish? What kind of friend would fake his death and think it was funny?

I was learning that friends have to do more than just answer phones or call you back. They have got to be prudent with their lives as well. This had been my third wake-up call relating to friendships, and I was moving on.

Love the soil

CHAPTER 6

Walking Home Shouldn't Be This Tough

Grammar school was almost over for the day. Home and fun were a little more than a mile away. I liked spending a few minutes during the last hour of each school day planning the trip home and what I'd do when I got there.

Julie was a year ahead of me in school and ready to head home as soon as the bell rang. I figured that if all went well, we'd be home before four o'clock, which left plenty of time to get something meaningful done before supper.

We walked at about the same speed and were about the same height, but I was much heavier than she. She didn't appear to eat a lot, and often just picked at her food; I, on the other hand, ate almost everything in sight.

Most days we took the long way home. Occasionally, we took a shortcut by cutting through my grandparents' backyard, passing their chicken coop, and scooting between the trees and into the field behind their house. I loved shortcuts. Julie was not at all fond of pucker brush and getting dirty, but since it shortened the trip home, she was okay with it.

I normally enjoyed walking to and from school. If you kept your eyes open, there was always something new to see. On this particular day, however, we chose to take the shortcut and about halfway home, as we turned the corner onto Franklin Street where we lived, I felt in my bones that trouble was coming.

Elgin lived on the corner of Franklin and Chamberlain Streets. For some reason, he didn't seem to like me. He attended a private school and arrived home earlier than we did.

Today was my lucky day. Elgin and his friends were there riding their bikes up and down Franklin Street, which had recently been re-tarred and then covered with sand. When the weather was hot, the tar seeped through the sand and stuck to your shoes. They pulled up beside us and began teasing us about not having bikes and still having to walk home from school. As usual, Elgin was very aggressive. Julie and I walked faster and tried unsuccessfully to ignore them.

I began to think that I wasn't going to play this game much longer no matter what the cost might be. I knew that one day something bad might happen with him, and I had tried to avoid it. I'd never had a fight before and didn't like the thought of one. At the same time, I didn't know how to ignore some of his straight lines. Then he said something stupid and, of course, I responded smartly.

He immediately stopped his bike in front of me. Then he jumped off, dropped the bike on the road, and said, "I am going to kill you."

His buddies gathered around, and Julie started screaming something at me as she headed up the road toward home. She appeared to be mad at me. What had I done? I encouraged her to go on home.

She screamed back, "I'll tell Momma and you'll be sorry." I figured she knew what was about to happen and was frightened for me.

Elgin took a swing at me, and we somehow grabbed each other. I was really spooked. He then got me in a headlock and tried to pull me to the ground. I didn't want my face rubbed in the sand and tar, so I pushed us to the edge of the grass. We stumbled down the embankment and into the shallow swamp water. I had my arm around his waist and was trying to hit him with my free hand. He wasn't that heavy but was about four inches taller than I was. I tried to get out of the headlock but couldn't, so I lifted him up in the air, and we both dropped into the water, which was only a foot or so deep. He let go and I was able to jump on top of him. For once, it was nice to be the heavier one. I grabbed his long arms and pushed them back over his head. What happened next was amazing!

Since Elgin and I were both of French descent, it didn't surprise me that his nose was as big as mine. *We may be related,* I thought, as I continued to hold his arms up over his head. As I did this, water ran into his nostrils. I watched it for a few seconds; I had never seen that before. When I let him up a little, he coughed and gagged. When I pushed him back down, the water ran into his huge nostrils again. I wondered how long it would take for his head to fill up with water.

He tried his best to get up, but I was too heavy and his arms weren't that strong. I had time to think, so I let him up a bit. He was screaming, coughing, gagging, and swearing in French. I pushed him down again, allowing a little more water to run into his enormous nostrils. But realizing that he could drown, I let go of his arms and rolled off him.

I had calmed down in the middle of it all. I felt like a new person. A huge weight had been lifted from my shoulders, and I felt free again. I knew that I would now be able to walk through this area as much as I wanted to and not be bothered by him again.

I looked around, and his buddies had disappeared. I watched him crawl up the embankment. Elgin picked up his bike and walked it home— crying and coughing at the same time. I saw him turn into his yard; then I headed home.

As I approached our house, I realized I was tired and that fighting takes an enormous amount of energy and is so out-of-control. I never started a fight and never will. However, once it starts, you have no choice. You must put everything you have into it or risk dying or getting seriously injured. I looked myself over. I was wet and dirty, but apart from having a bloody nose, I was fine. Thank goodness my books were still dry.

Since Dad worked second shift, I wouldn't have to deal with him when I got home, and Mom wouldn't overreact (at least I didn't think she would). I walked into the house and Julie pointed at me and said, "He started it. I told you, Mom, he started it." I still didn't think she was talking about anything but her fear that I'd be hurt.

Mom checked me over. "Go clean up and change your clothes. And don't forget to feed and water the chickens," was all she said.

She didn't usually talk a lot. I was glad she didn't chew me out, but I was a little sad because she didn't ask me anything about the fight. It was my first one; I wanted to share it with someone, but Dad was working and Julie was definitely out of the question.

I was physically tired but not ready to go to bed. The day had been too exciting for me to be sleepy. My dad sometimes brought a newspaper home from work at night and, if he hadn't finished reading it, left it in the dining room on a shelf under the radio. I usually looked for it in the morning, but since I wasn't sleepy, I decided now was a good time to read it.

The headlines read, "The State of Israel Is Proclaimed." The front page went on to say that David Ben-Gurion was named prime minister. It also said that President Truman immediately recognized the new Jewish homeland. That was amazing news to me. I'd heard some talk at school about the fighting in the Middle East but didn't realize Israel was now alive and well. What a historic event!

It shouldn't have amazed me because I had learned in Sunday school that the Bible promised Israel would be reestablished some day. It also talks about how the Lord will sometimes use what the devil intended to hurt His children to benefit them. If so many Jews hadn't suffered in Europe, I wondered if they would have escaped and reestablished Israel. The Bible says God's thoughts are not our thoughts.

I was getting sleepy. I said good night to Mom and headed to bed. Before I went to sleep, however, I thought a lot about Elgin. Would we be visited by his dad? Had I seriously hurt him?

I felt sorry for him as I relived in my mind every moment of the fight. All of his friends left him right when he needed them most. In reflection, I had learned a little about fighting and a little more about myself. I felt good about Israel and the fact that they now had a free country to live in like I had. The freedom to fight and win against anyone who wanted to push me or someone else around comforted me, and I dropped off to sleep.

A few days later I happened to walk by Elgin's house, and I saw him in his backyard. He saw me but quickly looked away. *Yes,* I thought, *the fight was worth it. I'm free at last!*

CHAPTER 7

Up and Down

Christmas was coming and so was the beautiful snow and ice. That was the good and bad news. It would be tougher to get back and forth to school, but the high potential of a few school days off due to "inclement" weather was exciting.

I loved that word *synonym*. *Stormy* meant lots of sledding; *rainy* meant more private time in the garage playing with my stuff; *windy* meant really hard ice and no wet pants from sliding on it; *foul* meant no one outside but the few, so it was peaceful and quiet; *rough* meant the impossible roads and more free time; *severe* meant stay home folks and be safe in this unpleasant but temporary weather.

Portland Street was nearly straight for almost a mile from just above its intersection with Guptill Street to the top of the first hill. At the top of that hill sat the Carters' farm. No, it wasn't my farm, but at times I wished it were mine. I skated on a small pond behind their farm and up the street a little, but that's another story.

That straight road was perfect for bobsledding. The Carter boys had built a bobsled, which was elevated over multiple runners. The sled had a ten-foot-long seat that sat about two feet off the ground with running boards halfway between the seat and the ground to place your feet on. The road runners were wood with metal bands protecting the wood from the occasional bare spots in the ice and snow. The front section was very short. Even though the car steering wheel that was welded to the stem and attached to front runners made it easy to steer, the bobsled was impossible to stop.

I never knew when they were going to take the sled out of the barn, so I just walked over and knocked on their farmhouse door and asked. Usually the youngest of the boys was ready to go but needed help pulling the bobsled out of one of the horse stalls and heading it down the driveway.

Five or six of us could sit on it and ride all the way down Portland Street. With only a short running start, we were on cloud nine as we sped down the street. We didn't feel that way about the long walk back up the hill though. It took all of us to pull the sled back up to the top of the hill. Many times we tried to hitch rides with people, but they just said, "No, no, no," and laughed.

Other than the city snowplows and a few milk trucks, there was hardly any morning traffic after nine o'clock. The snowplows almost stopped as we flew by and, if there was a car on the road, the driver always gave us plenty of room. Riding the Carters' bobsled was a dream.

As it got closer to Christmas, discussions about Santa and whether he was real or not filled the air at our house. Julie was locked onto his reality and convinced beyond a shadow of a doubt that he was real. She wanted a special doll for Christmas and was living a pure and sin-free life, believing that if she did, the doll would be under the tree at Christmas. She was also watching me every day for things she thought I was doing wrong. My parents dodged any questions and encouraged us to be good "just in case."

Sunday school didn't teach that Santa was real. All of the retail stores had it locked down though—he was as real as whatever you had left in your wallet. I was convinced that Santa couldn't exist because our chimney was too small. How could Santa be everywhere in the world on the same night? I don't think I ever even wanted to believe in Santa or the tooth fairy. They just didn't fit into my thinking.

I was quiet about my thoughts until Julie sounded off by saying something like, if Santa sees you doing that, you won't get anything for

Christmas. All I needed was another reminder of what I couldn't do right and how much I was going to pay for my mistakes.

Christmas came and there was no special doll under the tree for Julie. I found out later that Dad had determined it cost too much and had Santa provide her a less expensive doll, which looked pretty good to me. Julie went to her room and cried for two hours. No one could console her. It definitely put a damper on our Christmas.

I determined it wasn't the doll she was crying about but rather that Santa wasn't real to her anymore. She was so disappointed! She had to recover on her own even though Dad delivered the requested doll to her later in the week.

From that Christmas forward Julie wasn't quite as excited. As time passed and we both came to accept Christ as our Savior, her spirit was renewed, and she got more involved in celebrating the true meaning of both Christmas and Easter.

—⁂—

I loved the outdoors—both day and night. It was peaceful and guilt free. To me, the best place to be on a cold winter day just before dusk was sitting as high up as I could climb in the huge pine tree just behind the stone wall that marked the end of our garden. Deer and raccoons would come out of the woods at that time and dig in our garden for corn.

In the middle of winter, the bucks' coats were thick and their antlers fully formed. I loved to watch them lift their noses in the air and snort like they could sense someone was present but couldn't find them. *Kind of macho*, I thought. The coons didn't care. They could smell you if you were upwind. They didn't smell me because I was perched too high up in the pine tree.

It was okay to climb up the pine tree when the pine pitch was frozen. One time, however, it warmed up from my sitting so long in the tree and I ended up getting pitch all over me. I almost fell out of the tree trying to get it off my pants and hands. Gasoline was the only thing that removed the pitch and, according to my mother and sister, I smelled terrible. To me, it was still worth it, smell and all.

CHAPTER 8

Skater Tracks

There were no rivers or dams within a couple miles of our home. If you wanted to ice skate, you looked elsewhere. There was plenty of ice around, but it stayed frozen hard for only a few days.

Snow was everywhere, but so was the sun. The melting snow froze overnight and formed small frozen pools in the hay fields next to our home. Sometimes these frozen pools ran clear to our neighbor's farm. The ice wasn't just on flat farmland but also on the hills. The night freeze caught the melting snow as it ran down the hills below us and made narrow ice raceways where, for a few minutes, you could slide free of any effort.

My feet were too wide for figure skates, however, hockey skates were just fine. Julie and I loved to skate. We'd sit on our back steps in the early morning sun, put on our skates, and then climb through the barbed-wire fence that ran parallel to our driveway and next to an open field. In less than a minute's walk, we began skating on the narrow frozen pools of ice that seemed to stretch for miles.

The ice remained perfect until about ten o'clock; it was glorious. We raced, fell down on the ice, and slid for thirty to forty feet on our backs. Then the sun worked its damage on the ice, first along the edges where it became crunchy and then in the middle, creating pools of water. As the sun warmed the ice, our clothing got a little wet, but we continued to skate until we were soaked through. Then we walked home in crunchy semi-ice and snow. When we woke up the next morning, the ice ponds had been reshaped, and we'd do it all over again. Sometimes, the cow poop under the ice made for an assortment of colors and areas to avoid as the day warmed. The hay often stuck up through the ice and from a distance resembled seaweed along the ocean shoreline.

When the snow melted, we had to travel further away from home to ice skate. The Carters' farm was on Portland Street, which paralleled our street. Behind their farm was a small pond known by only a few skaters, hunters, thirsty cows, and horses. In total, the pond was about a half mile from our house. Depending on the weather, it could be either a neat, quick walk or a cold and tiring experience. The timing of the snowstorms determined whether the pond would be clear of snow or require an hour or more of shoveling.

One Sunday afternoon, I ventured out to skate at the Carters' minipond. I toted a shovel and had my skates tied together and hung around my neck. It was a beautiful day, and except for a few puffy clouds, the sky was clear and light blue. Because I'd behaved in Sunday school and church, I was free to enjoy the afternoon—unsupervised.

The walk to the pond was uninterrupted, and I was ready. Once I arrived at Portland Street and the farm, I climbed over the plow-formed snowbank and through the barbed-wire fence, and then trekked through the snow down along the row of trees and stone wall to the pond.

The pond was in a hollow where the surface water ran across the field and slowed as it was blocked by a stone-and-earth shallow dam. The water was no more than a foot deep, but the ice-covered pond was long and just wide enough to play hockey on, if you wanted to. I loved the quiet, cold privacy, as long as the sun was out and the wind wasn't blowing too hard. The crispness of the cold wind kept most people inside and left the open country to the few. It made me feel as though God had created this beauty just for me.

The afternoon went by too fast. Soon the sun was covered by clouds and the wind picked up. I figured I still had some time to skate, though not as much as I wanted. I skated for another half hour or more until it got too windy and began to snow. By then, the sun had gone down, and I couldn't see the rear of the Carters' farm anymore. I realized it was past time to go home. I'd made a stupid mistake.

My ice skate strings were frozen. I'd made double knots, as usual, and the snow had packed into the knots and frozen them solid. I couldn't untie them. I decided to wear my skates and carry my boots. After picking up the shovel, I said good-bye to the ice arena and headed along the stone wall and up the hill across the field.

Fifteen minutes later, I was still somewhere in the field and couldn't see the tree line or even ten feet ahead of me. The wind was blowing hard and the snowflakes were huge. I continued walking and kept looking for the trees and the barbed-wire fence I had to cross to get back to Portland Street.

I was getting cold and spooked. I didn't like chills, and I definitely had them. I didn't know whether the chills came from the snow and wind or were just activated by fear. Either way, I was ready to get home.

Now I was no longer walking in the snow. I was plowing through it on my skates, dragging the shovel and not moving very fast. Usually I loved my privacy, but now I wanted someone to speak to me and head me in the right direction. I was getting mad at my stupidity, and I was very cold. At seven, I didn't know the true meaning of the word "panic," but that's what I was experiencing.

My feet were the coldest part of my body. My skates didn't have the insulation my boots had, so I really needed to change them. *Never again will I leave the house without a jackknife!*—I said it over and over again. Never again will I stay past the time I need to find my way home.

I was making all kinds of commitments to myself and knowing I was going to start crying any minute. Saying a prayer quieted me down for a while. It became tougher and tougher for me to move through the snow—I was stone cold and really scared! I cried when I realized I was lost in the blowing snowstorm.

In the middle of my tears I heard my dad say, "What are you doing sitting there?" He was chuckling as he spoke.

With chattering teeth I tried to say, "Untying my skates."

"Let me take a look."

As he tried to untie the knots, I noticed that he was wearing his hunting hat, with the earflaps down, and the collar to his hunting jacket was up. He had taken off his buckskin gloves and was finally able to cut the frozen double knots. My feet weren't any warmer in my boots, but I knew they would soon warm up.

"Grab your skates and I'll take the shovel—let's go home."

We walked for about ten minutes. I couldn't hold back my question any longer, so I asked, "How did you find me?"

"You left a clear trail, Son."

I wanted to ask a lot more questions, but he was walking fast, and I had to focus on keeping up. The weather seemed better as we crossed Portland Street, and I was now bubbling with confidence. I was overwhelmed with my dad's rescue, as well as the fact I hadn't received a scolding. At that moment, I wanted to be just like Dad when I grew up.

The kitchen was warm and the hot bath was soothing. Sunday night supper was Welsh rarebit. That was fine with me—it was hot and good.

I decided that in the future I wouldn't skate alone or very far from home, and I'd definitely always carry a jackknife, no matter where I was or where I was going. There were so many lessons learned that day, and I knew I'd learned them without asking. It was one of my worst and yet best days ever.

CHAPTER 9

Doing the Fair Thing

Her name was Lucida. We were eight years old and in the third-grade class together at Guptill Elementary School. She was special. She had a sweet smile, a soft voice, bright eyes, and a nice laugh. She was always friendly and so easy to talk with. She and I walked or sat together at recess. I remember not having much to say most of the time, but that didn't seem to bother her at all. She said what she had to say quietly, and I enjoyed listening.

Lucida laughed at little things. Others in our class kidded us, but I didn't care. I just knew she was special, and I enjoyed being with her. I missed her company when we didn't spend time together at recess. She'd look over at me from a distance and smile that soft smile. I thought she was really neat.

Most days after school, we'd walk to the end of Guptill Street, say good-bye, and head to our own homes. Occasionally, I walked her all the way to her home and waited on her porch while she changed into her after-school clothes so that we could spend a little more time together. While waiting for her, I thought that there was just something warm and clean about her, no matter what she wore.

During one afternoon walk home, we kidded about kissing. I was interested and she may have been, but it didn't show. I knew somehow we were going to kiss, and the burden of when, where, and how was all mine. And I was lost.

Although I sometimes found being with her very exciting, I didn't have the guts to ask her for a kiss, nor was I going to sneak one—I wasn't that kind of guy. It was an awkward period. I needed to think more about how I was going to make kissing Lucida a positive event for both of us.

I don't know where it came from, but one afternoon I asked, "How do you feel about trading a kiss for a quarter?"

"I'll think about it," she replied. "See you next week."

I felt it was the fair thing to do, trade something of value to me—my lunch money—for something I was sure she'd value. But next week?

The weekend was quiet. I had time to think about Lucida, and I was apprehensive about Monday. I sincerely didn't want to do anything to hurt our friendship, so I had some regrets about my suggestion.

When Monday finally arrived, we both found ourselves too busy in the morning to say much. I skipped lunch and realized later in the afternoon that I was both hungry and nervous. When the school day was over, we walked slowly down the street together. My sister and one of her girlfriends were walking home ahead of us. They looked back and giggled. I imagined they were talking about us.

I slowed to a stop under a large elm tree. I looked around and noticed closed curtains in one of the houses and also that the elm tree blocked any visibility from the school. It was the right place. I took out my quarter and asked, "Do you remember our conversation of last Friday?"

Shyly looking down, she answered, "Yes, I do."

She looked up, puckered up, and kissed me. It was soft and okay. I was looking at her during the kiss. Her eyes were closed, and I wondered if she really wanted to kiss me or if it was just about the quarter. How stupid. I paid a quarter and couldn't even enjoy it. Next time it would be different!

I was very hungry and focused on what I'd find to eat at home. Supper was two hours away; so I went out to the garden and pulled some raw carrots, washed them off outside under the faucet, and ate them. That evening I attacked supper with a vengeance.

Later that week at recess, Lucida and I committed to meet after school. She never said a word as we walked down Guptill Street together. Lucida never asked for the quarter or thanked me for it. I took the lead and held out the quarter. She closed her eyes and we kissed. It was getting much better now that I was trying to relax.

As days passed, I learned to close my eyes and not think so much. I don't recall how many days I went without lunch, but I also learned to hustle home, pull more carrots, and drink lots of water. However, before my mother served supper I was usually washed up and sitting at the table hungrily waiting for food.

We continued to spend school breaks together, and sometimes I went over to her house after school. We were good friends and had fun doing simple stuff together. I don't recall us kissing any other time except under the elm tree.

School was more than a mile from my home. We didn't have a car and very few cars drove by our house. Some would say we lived in the country. We had a garden, fruit trees, and chickens. We had very little company other than relatives, and they always came to the back door. Pastors, salesmen, and strangers went to the front door. We opened the front door so seldom that opening it was a project.

One Sunday as my parents, Julie, and I sat in the combination dining and family room, someone knocked on the front door. The door had a curtain over the glass, so I couldn't see who it was.

When my dad opened the door, I was shocked to see Lucida's parents. They didn't see me, so I stayed away from everyone's view. As my parents and sister had never met them, they introduced themselves. I couldn't hear the conversation as they sat in the living room, but I sensed this was not going to be a good day.

It seemed as if her parents were there forever. I hoped Lucida was all right. I imagined all kinds of things. I couldn't figure out why they had come, but I knew it wasn't good news.

I finally heard the front door close and my dad calling, "Jacob." I headed for the living room. Lucida's parents had left. My dad's face wasn't red, so there was hope. He looked straight at me but didn't appear mad, nor did he say a word. My parents were playing it low key. *This,* I thought, *was new territory.* I didn't know how to react; therefore, I just shut up.

It was Mom who spoke up and asked, "Jacob, have you been going without your lunches?"

Hesitantly, I replied, "Yes."

"You know, we give you lunch money to keep you healthy." She continued, "We expect you to eat your lunch at school." As Mom spoke, Dad continued to look straight at me but never said a word.

I agreed not to trade my lunch money for kisses anymore and that was that. No loud scolding or anything. I was amazed! This was very unusual. My parents weren't subtle people, especially my dad. It didn't feel right but looked as if I was off scot-free—but little did I know.

When we returned to school, Lucida wasn't available to walk during recess and was cool in class. No soft smiles from a distance. I wondered what her parents had said to her that made her feel she should no longer be my friend.

What my mom had said to me made me want to talk to her as soon as I got to school. I wanted to share it and hoped she'd do the same. I assumed we'd both grow from the experience. Whatever her parents had said seemed to have driven a permanent wall between us. She didn't mentioned the event, and I felt so bad that I didn't want to bring it up for fear it would only make matters worse. I was finding out that a friendship with a girl was a very tough boat to keep afloat.

Based on Lucida's reaction, I knew she was concerned with more than my health. It had to have something to do with kisses and money, but I didn't get it. I didn't understand the significance of what I'd done. Nevertheless, I truly regretted my actions.

I watched her take a new path home after school that day. She walked through the back of the school yard, avoiding Guptill Street and the elm tree. She didn't look back.

Not too much later, I learned the implications of what I'd done and realized it could have destroyed her reputation. Whatever her parents told her had been the right words, at the right time, and obviously she had listened and learned.

I did not get off scot-free. I felt the results of my error every day Lucida and I shared a class together, even though we never talked about the elm tree events or her parents' visit to my home.

Lucida turned out just fine—no harm done.

Years later when I revisited my old neighborhood and drove down Guptill Street, I thought about Lucida and noticed that the elm tree was gone, but the memories of our few minutes were as clear as though it were just yesterday.

44

CHAPTER 10

Stronger than a Horned Pout

Uncle Ted, my mother's older brother, was tall like his dad, about six feet four inches, but much thinner. He and his family lived next door to my grandparents. I passed both homes as I walked to and from school.

My uncle was always kind to me. He treated me like a friend and not just a kid. When he realized I enjoyed working, he helped me find some work whenever he could.

He had a sweet nature, more like Grammy's than Grandpa's. He never embarrassed anyone or teased like Grandpa did. Uncle Ted appeared to have a servant's heart, and I'm sure that is why they elected him to be a deacon at our church. He was smart too. He worked as the assistant postmaster in our town's post office, which serviced about thirteen thousand people post–World War II.

Uncle Ted and Pepére, my paternal French grandfather, shared a mutual friend named Nathan. Fishing is what Nathan and Uncle Ted had in common. Whenever you saw Uncle Ted and Nathan together, you could predict what they were talking about.

Dad and Uncle Ted also enjoyed fishing together. Nathan, Uncle Ted, and Dad liked saltwater fishing in the Atlantic Ocean, as well as freshwater fishing in the numerous ponds and lakes nearby. They all lived close to each other; therefore, fishing together was convenient, inexpensive, and usually productive.

The three of them planned a one-night fishing trip for horned pout on a local lake. With Nathan's boat in tow, they drove to the lake, which was also used as a public drinking-water supply. It was okay to fish the lake, but swimming was not allowed. The chain-link fence around the lake kept most people away. The entire area had the appearance and feel of a nature preserve.

It was dark as they slid the small boat into the water. After storing all of their gear, they carefully climbed into the boat. Uncle Ted took the bow, Nathan took the stern, and Dad took the rowing seat. He slowly rowed to the middle of the lake where he stopped and lit up his pipe.

They all baited their hooks with worms from Uncle Ted's garden and prepared to enjoy a quiet night of fishing. Uncle Ted set the lantern near the side of the boat so that some of the light would reflect in the water, as this seemed to help attract horned pout.

Nathan hooked something quite strong. He couldn't reel it in without breaking the line, so he patiently worked the line until whatever he had hooked was tired. Then he reeled it in closer to the boat for Dad to net.

"It is huge," Nathan said, as he tried not to let it run too far with his line. "It has to weigh more than ten pounds!"

Ten minutes passed, and Nathan was bringing it closer to the boat so that they could see the catch under the lantern and net it. As it passed quickly under the boat and near the lantern on the other side, Uncle Ted caught the first glimpse of the freshwater eel and instantly instructed my dad to cut the line!

"Why? What did you see?" Dad asked.

"Just cut the line!"

Dad asked again, "Why, what is it?"

Nathan was busy trying not to lose it and couldn't see past my dad or into the water.

"It's an eel," said Uncle Ted.

"How big is it?" Nathan asked.

Dad suggested, "Let's get it into the boat and find out how big it is." He knew Uncle Ted didn't like snakes or eels or anything that crawled.

For the next few minutes, there was much discussion about the merits of keeping the eel out of the boat. However, at the same time, there were some convincing points made regarding the tasty flavor of properly cooked eel. If you've ever tried to hold a live eel, you'll understand why some people wouldn't like them.

Uncle Ted made it known loudly and clearly to everyone in the boat, on the lake, and in the county, that there was not enough room in the boat for him and that eel. Before the words cleared his lips, the eel flew up over the side and landed in the bottom of the shallow boat between Dad and Uncle Ted. It was flipping all over the place, and Uncle Ted saw that it was heading for his end of the boat.

New Hampshire lakes and ponds are cold and usually deep. By this time, all three of the men were standing up, and the boat was rocking back and forth. Suddenly, the boat jerked, and Uncle Ted was in the water headed for shore.

Dad and Nathan got untangled, caught the eel and unhooked it, and put it in the fish bucket. Everyone could swim well, so no one was worried about Uncle Ted not making it to shore. All went quiet again. Nathan and Dad watched as Uncle Ted walked along the shore headed for the car and boat trailer.

After the passing of a respectable amount of time, Uncle Ted talked to his buddies again. Nathan and Uncle Ted have since passed on, but my dad still laughs when he tells the story, recalling how exciting and funny it was for a few minutes in the middle of the lake that night.

Some say that Uncle Ted jumped out of that boat to avoid the eel. Others, professing they knew him better, claim that he fell out of the boat. Only Uncle Ted knew the real story. Either way, Uncle Ted was accurate when he said there wasn't enough room in that boat for both him and the eel.

Side note: Horned pout in New Hampshire look a lot like small catfish in the South—really ugly. They are black and have tentacle-like protrusions sticking out of their upper body. Nevertheless, they fry up well making a tasty breakfast with eggs and coffee in the morning on the lake. However, because they're a very bony fish, they need to be eaten slowly and cautiously.

CHAPTER 11

Teacher Needee

I recall that playing touch football at Guptill Elementary School was very informal but required speed and balance. The playing area had very little grass. It was mostly gravel spotted with lots of small rocks. You tried not to fall down or even touch your knees on the ground because the landing area was not soft and forgiving.

One day, I kicked a football off the side of my foot and through a second-floor window. The football took much of the broken glass with it into the teachers' rest area. I had been in that room a few times before at the specific invite of the principal, Miss Needee.

Miss Needee appeared to like pulling me around by my ears. Actually, it didn't make any difference if you were a boy or girl. She'd make some loud grunting noises, grab the nearest ear, drag you into the teachers' room, and lay down the law. Miss Needee was a combined fourth-grade teacher and grammar school principal. She was a large woman with strong hands and large feet. When she grabbed my ears, all I could see were those big shoes, and I did my best to avoid them.

Unlike Miss Needee, the first-grade teacher, Miss Lemoore, was beautiful in many ways. She appeared to enjoy her classes and her work. She was direct but sensitive and personal with all of her students. For some reason, I just blushed when I even thought about her. She had dark hair, light olive skin, and beautiful penetrating eyes. Miss Lemoore was not very tall, but tall enough, and she was a lady in every way; somehow I knew she was the standard I'd measure women against from then on.

The second-grade teacher, Miss Steel, was all starch. You couldn't crack a joke in her class about anything. You had to walk the line or go and see Miss Needee, the ear-grabber. Miss Steel must have sent me to see her twenty times. I was actually feeling sorry for Miss Steel by year end, and I still believe she graduated me just to get rid of me. She was neither a pretty woman nor was she happy in her job.

The third-grade teacher, Mrs. Voyager, was exciting. She involved each member of the class in the learning process and got me interested in geography and world history. She was tall and thin and always spoke so that you could hear her words clearly. Before she became a teacher, she traveled a lot. Her travel stories made it easy to imagine different parts of the world with their different cultures.

The sixth-grade teacher, Mrs. Champion, was, for some unknown reason, my advocate and made sure when I moved to junior high that I was placed in an advanced class. I seriously didn't know what she saw in me, but it enhanced my self-image and made me not want to disappoint her. I studied hard in her class and in junior high.

Thank goodness Mrs. Champion wasn't in the room when the football shattered the window. The football was never seen again by any of us who loved to play the game. The pieces of glass went down the back of Miss Steel's dress, or so I was told. She'd been sitting in front of the window, facing the center of the room, drinking coffee. She wasn't seriously injured but needed help removing the small pieces of glass from her back and dress. She went home after the incident to change and didn't return to school until the next day.

When the football hit the window, I believe Miss Needee immediately headed to the rear of the school looking for me. Having found me, she grabbed my ear and led me into the school to her empty classroom. She accused me of intentionally kicking the ball through the window when I realized Miss Steel was sitting in front of it, because everyone knew how I enjoyed antagonizing her. I was expelled until further notice.

Since we didn't have a phone then, she called the second contact person on the list, my grandmother. There was no answer there, so she instructed me to go home and not to come back until one of my parents could come with me.

My mom was home and listened to my story. Mom and Dad were different when it came to surprises. Dad at times blew up, but the next day it was forgotten. My mom almost never got mad but always remembered and usually got even.

The next morning, Mom and I walked to school together. I really felt bad about the inconvenience I caused her. Since she'd heard a few rumors about Miss Needee, she wanted to speak with her in person. I sat outside the teachers' room while they visited together. When the door opened, my mother's skin was white.

"Come, Jacob, let's go home!"

That was it. She didn't say much more on the way home. She was never a big talker, but I knew that wasn't the end of it. She and Dad had a long conversation before he headed out to start his second-shift job at two o'clock that afternoon.

Mom said, "Enjoy your day, Jacob. You won't be going back to school until your dad can go with you later in the week."

Wow, I thought, *free time. This can't get any better.*

Friday came and my dad walked me to school. While he met with Miss Needee, I sat in the same chair outside the teachers' room. This time it was different. I clearly heard their loud conversation. Dad was saying, "You will never touch him again, do you hear me?"

"No man tells me what to do," sharply replied Miss Needee. It went downhill from there.

The door opened and my dad called me into the room. "If she touches you again, you are to go straight home. Jacob, do you understand?"

"Yes, Sir," was my answer, With that, we all walked out into the hallway. Dad headed home and I went back to class.

Miss Needee left me alone for a while, but I walked on eggshells for a long time. It appeared that neither one of us wanted to trigger another event. When I got home each day, Mom would ask how school went, and I gave her honest answers.

Two years later, Miss Steel, my second-grade teacher, committed suicide. Ten years later, when it was my younger brother's turn to attend Miss Needee's fourth-grade class, my folks put him in private school. He returned to Guptill Elementary School and attended the fifth and sixth grades. My mother's doings, I firmly believe—she never forgot. Perhaps it was her way of protecting my brother as well as sending Miss Needee a special message.

Part of my mother's concern about Miss Needee's joy in pulling ears was not just the pain it inflicted on her sons. Grandpa had large ears that pointed slightly away from his head. According to my aunts, my mother tried to prevent my ears from looking like Grandpa's, as evidenced by her taping mine to my head when I was real little in an attempt to keep them from protruding or growing too large.

While in high school, I got better at kicking footballs and usually dated neat, dark-haired girls with olive skin and wonderful warm personalities. I've often felt bad about Miss Steel and wondered if I contributed to her misfortunes. I did, however, keep my eyes open all of the time for the Miss Needees of the world. As I got older, they were easier to spot, and I made an undying commitment to avoid them at all costs.

CHAPTER 12

A Toy Addiction

Guptill Elementary School was a three-story building with lots of tall windows. It was enormous compared to the homes around it. It was also unique and stood out, in that you could see parts of the building from every surrounding side street. It was as if you were unable to get away from it when the school day was over. You'd glance back and the building would still be in view.

Large trees lined the front walk. Our beautiful American flag waved high and proud on the flagpole situated on the school's lush, green, front lawn. It set the tone for the neighborhood. The place was special, and fifty years later it is still special.

The grounds on the left side of the building were a combination of dirt and gravel that gradually tapered to a six-foot chain-link fence. Behind the fence were some homes and a junkyard. On the right side of the school, the fence had a hitch in it where it opened up to an additional area. The combination of grass and sand on this side also tapered to the fence. From the rear, the building looked absolutely huge to me. It stood a full three stories and, at the same time, was similar to a home with a walk-out basement. I'm sure the ceilings on each floor were ten-to-twelve feet high. However, from the front, it looked like only a two-story building.

The walk-out basement had a door and many windows. The basement door led to an outside cement pad where girls jumped rope at recess.

This same area was protected from the wind in the winter and was a very popular place to congregate.

Inside the building, the classrooms were situated on the right and left sides with a wide hallway and stairway in the center. It resembled our city hall building with its tall ceilings and transom windows above each door, which, when opened, allowed air to flow into the room.

I loved to run up and down the center stairs. It was fun because the steps seemed to never end. You started out with someone next to you on the bottom step; when you hit the landing, they were either ahead of you or not focused. By the time you got to the second story, you were both laughing, no matter who got there first.

—⁓—

There was a material addition to the school during my second year. The new swing-and-slide set was as majestic as the school building. Many of us got chided as we anxiously watched the building process from our classroom windows. I'd only seen pictures of a swing-and-slide set, so the real thing was like something from outer space to me.

When the day came that the building project was completed and the workmen had left, I stayed after school and swung for hours. I went up and down the slide until I could do it on my belly, backwards, and upside down. I couldn't leave; I was addicted to the swing and slide.

It was dark before I realized that I hadn't thought about anyone or anything other than sliding and swinging. My grandparents lived about a half mile away and got out of work at four o'clock. They were so close by that I always felt safe in the neighborhood, so I wasn't too concerned about going home yet.

The nice thing about where they placed the new equipment was that it faced away from the junkyard yet was right in front of it. I was on the top of the slide and under the streetlights when I saw a police car drive slowly by the front of the school. I ducked down low on the slide and then headed for the junkyard fence, slid under it, and hid in the junk. After the police car left, I reentered heaven and continued my addiction.

It was fun swinging in the dark. You could see the streetlights in the distance and the sky was bright with millions of shining stars. I was flying on the swing and lost in my new world.

I never got tired, but I did become cautious. Every car that drove by either the front or back of the school got me off the swing and into the junkyard. I knew I was going to be in trouble, but what a small price to pay for the fun I was having.

Later, I noticed a large, dark something in the middle of the yard behind the school. It didn't appear to move like a bear or a big animal, but something was definitely there—it was hard to see what it was. I slowed my swing down. The moon was coming up in front of the school, so this thing was in the moon's shade in the rear of the building. This was making me uncomfortable. Again, I got off the swing and hid for a while in the junkyard. It didn't go away. I determined then that it was time to go home.

I didn't want to walk out in the open, so I tried to crawl over some of the junk but just couldn't do it. I was getting frustrated. To avoid being seen by whatever the big, black thing was about three hundred feet away, I'd have to go back under the fence and crawl along the bottom of it out to the front of the school. At first, I moved slowly, and then started to get up and run. As I did, bright lights went on and the car came towards me. I was caught.

My grandmother jumped out of the car and loudly called out my name. I felt saved, rescued, and relieved all at the same time. She was the only voice I wanted to hear when I was in trouble. Everyone else often called me Jake, unless they were mad at me. Then they would say Jacob. But Grammy always called me Jacob.

I got into the car and she drove us to her home. She didn't say much, other than to ask me to never do that again because it would hurt and worry my mom. I made a promise and kept it.

We didn't own a car, so Grammy was the one who searched for me while my mom stayed at home. I'm sure she kept things under control and knew just where to find me. She seemed to always know things that other people never discovered about her grandchildren.

When we arrived, there were other relatives in the kitchen talking to Mom. I got a big hug from her and then a lot of questions. I was embarrassed and felt so stupid and selfish. I told my mom that I was very sorry and glad they hadn't involved Dad. If they had called and gotten him out of work early, I might have been the unhappy recipient of a good whipping.

The following year, the school installed a jungle gym on the right side of the building. It was almost hidden in the ninety-degree corner of the fence that stretched from the front to the rear of the building. The jungle gym, which was about nine feet in diameter and eight feet tall, had a pull-up bar in the center, about two feet above the rest of the bars. The entire jungle gym was made of metal piping with smooth ninety-degree elbows and couplings. There was an inner circle and outer circle. It was fun to climb on but not something you could spend a lot of time doing—not like swinging. It was there, but not the focus of many of the older students.

Seth Richards was the smallest student in our class, and he loved the jungle gym. If he was not in class, he was on it. Seth was a bright guy, so I couldn't understand what attracted him to the jungle gym. Then one day, I noticed a group of guys gathered on it. I walked over and hidden in the middle was Seth sharing a cigarette with some students in the next grade. I liked Seth. Later that week, he shared a cigarette with me. I'd smoked some of my dad's before, so it wasn't a big deal.

It was getting colder. You could feel winter coming on. The afternoon recess bell had been rung, but I was slow to head back to class. Something was bothering me. When I looked back over my shoulder and through the chain-link fence, I saw something hanging very still on the jungle gym. It looked to be hanging on the inside ring, but from that distance it was hard to figure out just what it was. I knew my teacher, Miss Needee, was going to chew me out if I didn't get a move on, but something told me to check out the jungle gym.

I jogged back to it. As I got closer, I saw that a small person was hanging from the center pull-up bar. I couldn't believe it! It was Seth. His whole body was wrapped in his oversized jacket; he was hanging by the rope in his hood, which had been tied to the top bar. His hands were in his coat pockets, and the jacket band, normally tied around his waist, was tied around his arms and above his waist.

I climbed through the outer ring and got under Seth. I lifted him up on my shoulders and held him against the top inside bar. While he rested on my shoulders against the bar, I tried to untie the hood rope. He wasn't making a noise and the rope was almost impossible to untie from where I was standing. It finally let go, dropping us both to the ground. His face was white—I was sure he was dead. I pulled him through the bottom bars out into the open area and untied his jacket. Seth was breathing now, and slowly his face turned from white to a light pink.

His first words were, "Please don't tell anyone, please!"

I asked, "Who did this and why?"

He told me that some guys in the next class were upset because he wouldn't give them his cigarettes, so they said they'd teach him a good lesson. He thought that if we reported them, the principal would find out he'd been smoking and selling cigarettes, and he'd be in big trouble.

He said, "Thanks for saving my life."

What amazing words those were; I was overwhelmed. I liked Seth before he was hung. He had said the magic words. Now I liked him even more. After that, I walked him home a few times and even met his family and neighborhood friends. None of them knew about our shared experience.

While at his house one day, a beautiful girl walked by. She said, "Hi" and walked on.

She looked like a miniature version of my first-grade teacher. She had dark hair and a fair complexion. I thought that she might be of French descent, but Seth said she wasn't. He mentioned she went to a private school. I thought she had the right look, but the timing wasn't good. I was there to be with Seth and couldn't just go off and chase some girl I'd never met—but she sure looked very special.

However, a few years later when I was biking through the area, I saw her again. This time she was pregnant. What a disappointment—so young! Looking back, I realized that the timing was better than I had initially realized.

I've often reflected on that day and Seth. I have concluded that God had decided it wasn't Seth's time to enter heaven. In addition, I read somewhere that when you save someone's life, you'll always feel responsible for that person. If asked, I'd say there really is some truth in it. It's hard to believe, but Seth is the first person I ask about when talking to former classmates and the first person I look for at school reunions.

CHAPTER 13

Chasing Forgiveness

The A & P Grocery store in our town had aisles of tall shelves stacked high with food. I recall the smell of fish as my dad led me past the fresh fish counter during our periodic store visits. The several checkout counters seemed as high as the car windows and walking between them felt similar to walking between two buildings.

During one of our shopping visits, I spotted a ten-dollar bill lying on the floor. It was in the mid-40s, and my dad hadn't been home from overseas long, so that was a lot of money.

I picked it up and asked the cashier, "Is this yours?"

"Yes," he said and thanked me.

I looked up into my dad's eyes and I saw something, but it wasn't admiration. Dad picked up our bags of groceries and led me outside. Once outside and away from the store, we stopped.

He leaned down and said, "Son, I want to teach you something." He didn't say that often, so this was serious. I could feel the tension. I was a little spooked, but listened carefully.

"When you find something," he said, "remember this honorable principle: it is finders keepers; losers weepers."

He explained what it meant and reviewed my actions relative to the ten dollars I gave away. He complimented my desire to be honest, but emphasized something found may be a gift to keep. He never mentioned it again.

As days passed, I kept thinking about the ten dollars and decided to ask my mom how much ten dollars was worth. She explained that it was about what Dad earned each day when he went to work. I looked at her with an expression like, "that helps a lot." So, she went on to say that if Dad wanted to buy a new dress shirt, he might be able to buy four or five of them with ten dollars. Then she asked me if that helped, and I told her it did. But in truth, it made me feel much worse.

—⚬⚬⚬—

Along New Hampshire country roads, a walk is usually quiet except for the sounds of birds and the wind passing through tall trees. The traffic is infrequent, and you usually know most of the folks who drive by. Some of the trees and groups of bushes along the walk become familiar distance markers and bring on the feeling of relief as you get closer to home.

Daydreaming came easy to me during those walks. I often thought about the ten dollars that I gave away years earlier. It seemed that every time I was broke the incident came to my mind.

On this particular day, I remembered our Sunday school teacher repeating what Christ had said about faith. It was something about how a small amount of faith could move mountains. I wondered if I had enough faith to find money along the side of the road. If faith was a matter of believing in Christ as my Savior, I knew I had enough of that kind of faith. So, I thought, it couldn't be as simple as just acting on my faith by looking for money on the side of the road, could it? Since I was broke again and had to walk home anyway, I decided to search the grass along the side of the road for money, with the belief in my heart I'd find something.

As I walked, I asked God to help me find some change. I didn't have rich taste; some silver would do me just fine. After walking about an eighth of a mile from the stop sign on Franklin Street and heading toward home, there it was—a one-dollar bill half hidden in the sand and weeds. I was amazed!

How could it be, I wondered, *that God would help me find a dollar bill?* A dollar could buy five to six loaves of bread or a gallon of milk. It was a lot of money to me. I would have been happy with much less. I thanked

Him for the gift, but also realized that my experience was about more than just money.

Like many others, you may believe that my find that day can be explained away as the result of the focused efforts of a young boy searching for a lost buck. That thought crossed my mind, but it was more personal to me. It was a subtle confirmation that life was more than what we see and feel. It was about the possibility of a relationship with someone who can and will respond to the faith of a child.

—⁂—

Someone at school had repeated a story to me about a young boy who asked a stranger for a donation to a children's home. As the story goes, the good-hearted stranger handed the boy a small donation, and as the boy was walking away with the money, the stranger asked him, "What is the name of the children's home?"

"Mine," was his response.

An interesting story, I thought.

On the way home one day, I saw our neighbor, Dakin Walker, up ahead and thought about the story. Mr. Walker, being who he was, preferred that everyone just call him Dakin, so we did. I'd seen Dakin many times before walking up and down Franklin Street. Sometimes he walked straight and sometimes not so straight. He always seemed to wear the same old clothes.

He lived in a shack at the top of the hill across the street from his family's farm. The building he lived in resembled a large chicken coop. The windows were so dark that you couldn't see anything inside. There was an old Ford Coupe parked behind the building. It was a beautiful car but was never cleaned or used. I felt sorry for Dakin. He seemed to be a nice guy but was living in a deep, dark, lonely rut.

My dad told us Dakin was a part-time painter and a full-time drunk. He shared that Dakin's sister ran the farm and wouldn't let Dakin live in the house because of his drinking.

On a clear day, the view from the farm and Dakin's cabin into the valley was magnificent. I loved to ski the hill next to Dakin's place when the snow was deep. When it wasn't deep, it was fun to ride a sled down the hill on the frozen ice. Franklin Street appeared to cut right through their farm. I wondered many times if they had wanted it that way or not.

On that particular Friday, Dakin was weaving back and forth as I caught up to him. We talked as we approached the hill, and then I did it. I asked if he would like to donate money to a children's home. He looked at me from under his old, dirty hat.

He said, "I only have fifty cents."

"That's fine," I replied, and he handed me his last fifty cents.

"Thanks," I said, and started to run ahead.

"What's the name of the children's home?" he questioned.

"Mine," I hollered back and ran faster.

Saturday was a blur, but Sunday was payday. We attended Sunday school and church and sat down for a wonderful Sunday noon meal. We called the Sunday noon meal *dinner*, as most did in New Hampshire, and we always enjoyed having Dad at the table with us. Because he worked the second shift during the week, we didn't have many big meals together as a family. In the middle of the meal, we all heard a loud bang.

Dad said, "You all stay here." He got up from the table and ran outside and down the street toward the farm next door.

We slowly finished our meal and waited for Dad to return. Hours passed and we were sitting down for a light meal of soup and sandwiches when Dad finally walked up the driveway. We heard him come in, wash his hands, and then he sat down and joined us for supper. I asked what was up, and he told us Dakin had shot himself in the mouth with a shotgun. I was shocked and started to cry. I could feel my dad, mom, and Julie watching me.

Dad said, "Wipe your nose and don't worry; Dakin may be better off. He was fighting a losing battle with booze." What my dad said didn't make me feel any better. I knew in my heart that I had taken Dakin's last fifty cents just two days before.

Dad recalled the story of Dakin breaking our front door window while trying to warn us of a forest fire prior to its passing by our home. He mentioned that if Dakin had been sober, he would have come around the back as he always did. I felt weak, almost sick, and cried again.

Dad asked, "What is your problem?"

I told him that it was my fault Dakin killed himself; I shared how I had taken Dakin's last fifty cents. For a few moments there was total silence. Then, trying to comfort me, Mom said, "We all make mistakes."

Dad continued by sharing that Dakin had bigger problems than the fifty cents. He said, "Dakin was really sick and there was nothing anyone could do to help him. I'm sure that what you did had nothing to do with his death."

It seemed that all of the things I'd done wrong in my life before this paled because I could never apologize to Dakin and make it right. What a miserable lowlife I was no matter what Mom and Dad said. I felt as if I'd never be forgiven for this one. Dakin was gone, so who'd forgive me?

During the next few days, I reflected on my stupidity, including the time I used a small can of gasoline to start the boiler fire that had gone out. I was supposed to keep coal in the boiler so that the fire wouldn't go out. But, it had. When I couldn't get it started with paper and small pieces of wood, I went to the garage and got some of the gasoline we used in the cultivator and poured it into the boiler. I almost blew up the house. How could I be so stupid? Why couldn't I ask people for help?

I couldn't get over Dakin. I had to find a way forward, but nothing was working. I sat on the cellar stairs in the dark thinking about the alternatives. In my heart I knew I was a bad kid. I felt that what I'd done to Dakin was unforgivable. The Bible says, "Eye for eye ..." (Exodus 21:24), and that to me meant my life for his life.

With that thought, I took one of Dad's razor blades and held it in my hand. Sitting there on a cellar stair, I laid it across my wrist and wondered how long it would take to bleed to death. I read somewhere that you'd pass out before that happened.

I didn't really want to die, but I couldn't get rid of the guilt. I looked over to the shelf next to the stairs and noticed my dad's army boots sitting there. The toes of the boots were turned up a little, and I wondered how many miles he must have walked in those boots to get home safely. How had my dad survived fighting in the South Pacific? Then and there, I decided that since he had handled that, I could find a way to get over my guilt.

Sunday school and church were social events to me and nothing more—until Dakin. Sunday came and I listened closely to the pastor when he talked about Christ's forgiveness and how someday we might come to a point in our lives when we can't forgive ourselves for something we have done. He described how Christ had taken our past, present, and future sins to the cross with Him when He was crucified. He said from that point on, that God, the Father, no longer remembers our sins; it's as if they never happened.

I felt something I'd never felt before—the hope of being free of guilt. I knew it was time to invite Jesus into my heart and to surrender my sins to Him—including what I'd done to Dakin—and trust that what the Bible said was true. I didn't want to carry this any longer. I needed it off my back, and needed forgiveness.

I was standing next to my dad when the pastor invited anyone who wanted to surrender their sins to Christ that day and receive salvation to come forward. I stepped away from my dad and out into the aisle and walked to the front. I accepted Christ as my personal Savior that day. There were tears in my eyes when the pastor held my hand and said, "Let's pray for Jacob together."

No one made a big deal of what happened in church on Sunday. That was fine with me because I knew that from that day forward I'd never be the same. I knew that God had forgiven me for all of my stupidity, including what I'd done to Dakin.

I really believe I was Dakin's last straw, and that God used that event in my life to bring me to Him. I believed then and believe now that I am God's adopted child through Christ's sacrifice on the cross. Thanks to Christ, I have been at peace with my stupidity ever since.

Learning the basics at church

CHAPTER 14

Managing Conflict

While in grammar school, I participated in a school play. I wore my grandfather's suit, which was ten sizes too big for me. Many students from each class participated, so lots of parents attended. All things considered, the play went well.

The producer of the play was our outgoing third-grade teacher, Mrs. Voyager. She had traveled much and knew a lot about what went on outside New England. She focused the play and participants on geographic social differences and used humor to teach us how those differences could become undeserved prejudices.

In the play, I was a noble farmer trying to keep up with the Joneses. The play exhibited the memory skills of some and the acting skills of others. It was a wonderful learning process for many of us. I was impressed with the performance of some of the students, especially those who'd never impressed me before.

During this same time period, I was trying to learn how to play the trombone at school. My lessons were on Wednesday, so I carried the encased trombone to and from school on those days. I found that carrying the horn was much easier than learning to play it.

On the way home one Wednesday afternoon, Buck Jones, a sixth grader, was standing at the end of the school walk. As I passed, he made a remark about me being some kind of a duck out-of-water in the play and further commented on how tired he was getting of listening to me trying to blow my horn while he was serving detention down the hall.

I wondered why Buck would be waiting for me just to share this kind of stuff. Who cared what he thought, although I had to agree that my horn playing sounded terrible. He tried to grab my trombone case, and then we went at it.

I immediately had a bloody nose, but we each managed to get in a few good hits. I wasn't emotionally into the fight, and I'm sure I absorbed more pain than he did. I wasn't mad at him and really didn't want to fight. Didn't this guy have better things to do than wait outside just to start a fight? We finally stopped fighting and after a lot of verbiage went our own way, but not before he promised to be waiting for me the next day after school.

When the next afternoon came, I looked out the window a few minutes after the bell rang and saw that most of the students had already left. But there he was, waiting as promised. Again, I wondered what was wrong with this guy.

Miss Needee, the principal, asked, "What are you still doing here?"

I figured that there was no sense in soliciting her help. I grabbed my books and went to the basement and rested on the king's throne for ten minutes while thinking about what to do. Picking up my books again, I headed for the front door. Buck was still there waiting for me and in serious need of something he thought I could provide.

"I told you I'd be waiting!" he said.

"What's wrong with you?" I asked.

"I just don't like you! You think you're something special, so I'm going to teach you that you're not."

I knew I wasn't anything special, but what was it to him anyway? He was leaving me no choice. *Lord, what is it I have to do to get this guy off my back?*

He took a swing at me and then a second one. The fight was on. We punched and wrestled until we were at the street corner. We weren't hurting each other with the punches enough to stop the fight, so I pushed him into a hedge of bushes. I had the weight advantage and had learned a year or so ago on Franklin Street to use it as leverage. I pinned him down in the prickly bushes, and he screamed to be let up—the back of his neck and head probably hurt from the broken branches.

I told him I'd let him up on the condition that he left me alone from now on. He finally agreed, and I let him up. But once out of the bushes, he informed me that he and his brother, Buster, would be waiting for me Monday after school. He then turned and headed home.

Wonderful, I thought, *from the frying pan into the fire.*

My dad and I discussed the subject Saturday night and his conclusion was that I had no choice but to be ready to finish it.

I asked, "What do you mean by finishing it?"

"He's got to respect you enough to leave you alone, no more than that. Are you ready?"

"I'm not sure," I said.

He went on to tell me the simple truth. The only way to make Buck respect me was to put him on the ground and to do it again and again until he stayed there. We went down to the basement and walked over to the hanging punching bag, and he slowly showed me what to do. He suggested I keep working the bag and practice what he'd taught me. I stayed there and worked at it for two hours. I had lots of stamina, just no fighting skills. The key was setting up the power punch. The process included patience, timing, and putting my weight behind the punch. I worked the bag again on Sunday, both in the afternoon and evening.

Monday came and I thought a lot about what my dad had said—that winning a fight was more of a head set than physical strength. I wasn't looking forward to Buster joining the party and really had no idea if he would even show up.

On Monday as I walked out of school, the brothers were both there at the end of the walkway. I was starting to get very upset; I'd really had enough of this game.

Buck said, "I told you he'd be here and you are in for it now."

As Buck came at me, I held back and waited. He swung and missed, and I quickly hit him in the mouth as hard as I could. I tried to put all of my weight behind the punch. Buck went down—then he grabbed his chin and got up again.

Buster just stood there and said nothing as Buck came at me again. I waited and hit him in the nose as hard as I could, again with my weight behind the punch, and he dropped to the ground grabbing his bleeding nose. He got up and stood bent over in front of his brother.

They both walked off saying nothing to me, but talking to each other. I was amazed! Not a word from Buster. *Is that what Dad meant by respect,* I wondered?

Buck and I didn't speak until years later when we ran into each other downtown. He had quit school and was working construction somewhere and was home for vacation. He wanted me to know that he'd been working out and asked if I wanted to try him again now.

"Thanks Buck," I said. "I've nothing to prove, do you?" and then we parted.

—⟋⟋⟍—

I'd like to be able to say that Buck was the last person I fought with in grammar school, but it wasn't. Fern was a year behind me in school and large for his age. He was a pusher and made it a point to push kids around in the school hallway. He was like a roving bull looking for someone to knock down. It was unusual because he was smart and likeable most of the time. I guessed he just had bad days. He pushed me once, and I told him to knock it off.

Later, as we walked down the street, he pushed me again. I pushed him back. He took a swing at me, and I did the same. I had my usual bloody nose, and he a red cheek. I thought we were friends and had no desire to hurt him. As I started to walk away, I looked up and there was my dad driving my grandmother's car. I approached the car and he asked, "Where do you think you are going?"

"Just getting in the car, Dad," I said.

"You haven't finished the fight," he said. "Go finish it!"

I liked Fern, but Dad was Dad, and I had to finish it. So back to Fern I went. Fern helped by asking, "Back for more, stupid?"

I waited, and he finally walked into it and down he went. I walked to the car and got in. Fern got up and headed home. It was over and I'd had enough fighting for a lifetime.

I found that finishing the fight took focused emotion. I had to get really mad to hit someone hard enough to knock them down. In reality, I just wanted to get on with life. But what was there about me that motivated guys to pick a fight with me? Whatever it was, I committed to myself to figure it out and change.

Like many other people, I did figure it out but decided not to change. I realized I didn't like being intimidated or pushed round. In addition, I was a smart mouth. When someone said something challenging, I couldn't shut up. I responded with a remark I thought was funny—it was just too tempting. With these few winning experiences, on Friday nights I watched professional boxing on television through my neighbor's window (that is, as often as they'd let me). The greatest fight that year was the battle between Rocky Marciano and Jersey Joe Walcott.

Rocky came from our part of the country and was drafted and served in the US Army for two years during World War II. With his right cross, the one my dad had taught me, Rocky knocked out Jersey Joe in the thirteenth round. Rocky had been knocked down in the early part of the fight and was behind in points, but nothing stopped him. He waited for the right time and popped Jersey Joe. Just like my dad said, fighting is more brain than muscle. It was Rocky's first World Championship, and he went on to become the only World Heavy-Weight Champion to stay undefeated.

With Rocky as a role model, I decided one way or another to stay undefeated for the rest of my life. I never looked for or ever started a fight. But I worked hard at staying in shape and maintaining stamina, just in case. I also became very selective of where and with whom I spent my time. So far it has worked.

CHAPTER 15

Shared Gene

I f you have visited the countryside in any New England state, you've seen all kinds of old farms. Many of them, which were built prior to motor vehicles, are divided by the roads that pass through them. It appears that the farm buildings, including the barns, were built at a distance from the main house. This seems smart considering animals were in the barns and outer buildings, and with the summer heat, no one sleeping in the farmhouse wanted to be downwind.

It follows that roads started out as horse-and-buggy trails to and from the farms. These trails were natural cuts between the buildings and later became public roads. For those growing up in New England, this seems normal, but for outsiders it may appear odd to watch a farmer wait for traffic to pass so that he can drive his truck or tractor from one part of his property to another.

This picture describes the farm next to our home in New Hampshire. It was a large farm at one time, but it had seen its best commercial days. The farmhouse, barn, and outbuildings were stained brown and surrounded by beautiful, mature hardwood trees. The main house had a large front porch facing the road that divided the farm. One could easily visualize the original owners sitting comfortably on the porch in the evening enjoying the setting sun. Although the farm was old, it still reflected its strong character, unique personality, and continued functionality.

The fields were fenced with barbed wire to keep the few cows and large bulls inside. I'd go near the bulls, but I never baited them. The cows were different; they seemed to like being talked to and handled.

The original owners had died and left their daughter in charge of the farm. They had had two sons, Jake and Dakin, who were quite different. Jake still lived there with his sister. He was crippled but still drove the tractor that cut the hay. The hay was baled each year and Jake managed the workers when they came to help harvest all of the fields.

Jake had one immobile leg that he dragged around. The leg was in a brace under his pant leg and he'd lift it with one hand to get on and off the tractor. When he was off the equipment, he used crutches to get around. He was thin and short but had a lot of upper body strength.

Jake was always busy working on the farm. He'd remove one of the rear tractor wheels and use it to power a wood-cutting saw. The cut wood was split and used for heating the house and shed during the winter. He was friendly and enjoyed my company. I loved being with Jake on the farm. From the smell of wood being cut to the smell of hay being harvested, I enjoyed it all.

There was an enormous lump on Jake's forehead, right above his eye. My biggest challenge when I was with him was to not look at his lump, which stuck out more than an inch from his head. I didn't know what it was, but I prayed, "Lord no matter what I do wrong during my life, please don't let one of those lumps grow on my forehead."

I don't know why I didn't pray to be healthy or to not be crippled like Jake. I just prayed the prayer about the lump on his forehead. Jake was a great guy. He worked hard from dawn to dusk in spite of his handicap and had done his best to help his alcoholic brother.

Life is wonderfully unpredictable! I grew up and one day, I looked in the mirror and what did I see growing on my forehead just above my right eye but a lump. I immediately thought about him. I couldn't believe it. I was growing a lump just like Jake's. Was it the water? Did it come from the soil? Was it in the corn?

I had learned since being with Jake that God doesn't punish His children, so I knew God didn't put it there to punish me. I also believed that God had let it grow there to benefit me somehow. My job was to figure out what God wanted me to learn from this shared gene.

I visited the doctor and he told me it was a "fatty tumor that grew on the skull bone." That made all the difference in the world. Jake and I shared the fatty tumor gene and mine was currently growing on my skull. I learned that once removed it could come back at any time, and it did. Since having three removed from my forehead, I've grown to respect the tenacity of Jake's gene.

Frequently I've looked for lessons in this shared gene. I came up with three reasons why I believe the Lord allowed Jake to share his gift with me:

1. To remind me of Jake and his courage and commitment to his family by taking care of the farm in spite of his disabilities.

2. To keep me focused on maximizing the use of my physical capabilities as Jake did.

3. To always keep me thanking God for the blessings of a healthy body.

As we'd say today, Jake was one of the many million unsung disabled heroes in America doing the impossible with their limited physical resources.

CHAPTER 16

Fun Lessons

The small lakes in New Hampshire are unusually clean and clear. They are also very cold year-round. Fishing wasn't my thing, but my grandfather Pepére took me along just the same. During my youth, Pepére owned two different boats.

His high-speed runabout had a large outboard motor on it with opposing pistons. It ran like the wind as he raced it back and forth across a small lake in the neighboring town of Milton. I sat in the front seat, my eyes watering from the wind, and enjoyed the excitement. I didn't know at the time, but the love of being in and on the water was growing in my veins.

If Cub and Boy Scouts had involved boating, I would have stayed with them longer. Camping in the parks and swimming in the lakes around the parks was fun, as long as it didn't include bloodsuckers. Some people call them leaches, and one lake, in particular, was full of them. The only fun was throwing them in the campfire and watching them explode like firecrackers. Because they were full of blood, you didn't want to be too close.

Pepére eventually sold his high-speed outboard for a large inboard fishing boat made for deep water. The boat had room for five or six people. It had a canvas cover with steel ribs holding it up and a front window that could be closed up in case of rain. The Gray Marine inboard engine had only 16 horsepower, but it pushed the boat faster than the incoming or outgoing tides at Dover Point, and that was what counted.

Dad and Pepére loved to fish, and when I was invited along, I'd steer the boat. Fishing wasn't interesting to me, but I could steer the boat for hours and not be bored.

Pepére feared very little; I liked that about him. He moored his fishing boat on the Piscataqua River, which was fed by two large rivers in southeastern New Hampshire: the Salmon Falls and the Cocheco. The tide's dangerous currents in the Piscataqua River were apparently well known by most residents of the immediate area, but not by me. The river divides New Hampshire and Maine as it approaches the Atlantic Ocean. Pepére asked me to row his small rowboat to where the larger boat was moored in the river.

I listened closely to Pepére when he told me how to angle the rowboat upstream enough as we crossed the river to enable us to drift down to his fishing boat and catch it as we floated by. It was physically challenging trying to row against the river's tide currents. The water swirled and tried to take control of the boat many times as I pulled the oars hard to keep us headed in the right direction. We finally caught the boat's anchor line and pulled ourselves tight against the moored fishing boat. My heart was thumping loud enough for me and anyone close by to hear it.

When we returned from our day of fishing, the tide was headed in, so it didn't take us long to reach Pepére's moored rowboat. He hooked the mooring line with a fish gaff while I kept the fishing boat in reverse. The mooring line was attached to a chain that was attached to an old car engine lying on the bottom of the river. While we fished, Pepére told me that the mooring engine had pipes running through the pistons' cylinders to hold the engine in the muddy bottom.

I wasn't as excited about rowing back to the dock as I'd been about rowing out earlier that morning. I didn't want to let Pepére down, and I could see that the current was stronger than it had been earlier in the day.

It took us awhile to put all of our stuff in the rowboat and tie the canvas down on the fishing boat. Pepére told me that it wasn't safe to leave anything of value on a moored boat because it would be stolen. He went on to say that mooring was free, but the work of getting to and from the boat, plus having to haul everything back and forth, made you wish it were docked somewhere.

We piled our fish bucket, poles, and other stuff into the rowboat and took our seats. I took a deep breath. Pepére sat in the stern; I sat in the rowing seat. He reminded me that the incoming current was faster than the outgoing current had been that morning, and that I needed to take a bigger angle downstream so that the current wouldn't push us past the dock.

"I know," I said under my breath, as I was getting a little spooked.

Again, I didn't want to let him down. You guessed it—Pepére let go of the mooring line and his fishing boat, and we were off. I pulled the oars deep and fast, thinking that I was headed downstream enough to prevent the current from turning the bow of the boat.

Pepére hollered loudly, "We're not headed at a deep enough angle." So I pulled harder against the current.

"Not enough," he said. I pulled even harder, but it seemed as though we were headed back out to the ocean.

"Not enough," he repeated again.

Now, I was at full throttle. The current was not only pushing us upstream but trying to turn the bow of the boat. I looked straight into Pepére's eyes for a second and knew he wasn't worried, just focused. I pulled even harder against the current and kept rowing. I'd never seen him excited, but today, I thought, he was.

He looked right at me and said seriously, "You don't want to miss that dock, Jacob, or we'll end up in the fast currents under the bridge, and that could be dangerous."

I gave it all I had and started to sweat. I felt myself getting mad. It was like being in a fight. Forget how hard it was a second ago, just do it better and do it faster.

"Row harder, faster. Do it! Do it! We're almost there," he excitingly commanded.

I couldn't see anything other than Pepére looking past me at something. I knew that if I took the time to turn and look, we'd fail to keep our speed and angle. Pepére was depending on me to row; I was depending on his eyes and his judgment.

"Drop the oars and grab the dock, now!" he hollered.

I turned quickly, lifted my leg over the seat and leaped; I grabbed the corner of the dock and held on for dear life. Pepére came up behind me just as quickly, grabbed my legs and kept me in the boat. I thought the bow of the rowboat was going under the water, but fortunately it didn't. Together, we pulled and positioned the rowboat close to the dock and out of the main river's current.

I tied the bow of the boat to the dock and then rested against the dock, completely out of breath. I looked over at Pepére. He was sitting in the bow, catching his breath. We caught the look of relief in each other's eyes and both burst into laughter.

We stacked everything that was in the boat onto the dock and then pulled the boat out of the river, turned it over, and tied it down on the trailer. We then packed the car with all of our gear, including the oars, and headed to Portsmouth for supper.

I took a quick last look at the Sarah Mildred Long Bridge and watched the incoming current hit the tall bridge-support beams and then splash back into the water. I got a chill thinking we could have been doing the same thing.

On the way to the restaurant, we stopped at a small grocery store/bait shop where Pepére purchased some ice and filled the bucket, covering the fish we had caught and cleaned. The hot food, warm restaurant, and his company were all special. We talked about the day and laughed again and again about the close call. I don't think Pepére ever shared our experience with my dad, or else I would have heard about it. It was a good experience—I liked being part of a successful team.

Some people, like Pepére and Grammy, had a way of helping you learn from mistakes, while at the same time not putting you through a lesson in public humility. I hoped that I, too, would become that kind of friend and parent.

Pepére, my French grandfather

CHAPTER 17

Recreation

Family reunions were always a blast at Grammy and Grandpa's house. There was space enough for everyone to park, eat, socialize, and take a nap, if necessary. Their four children and their spouses, nineteen grandchildren, and distant uncles, aunts, and cousins were invited. It was always potluck with every family bringing their homemade favorite foods, as well as stories and pictures to share with everyone.

There was no dark side to the reunions. We all pitched in. Preparation for each reunion had started weeks before and cleaning up after each event went quickly because everyone joined in. The two most important and frequently used facilities were, of course, the upstairs and downstairs bathrooms.

Usually, there were organized games in which everyone either participated or watched. At other times, the recreation was as simple as just sitting together and sharing. Sometime during the event, everyone caught up on family news, and often this was defined as things that we children were not supposed to know. We learned more about our immediate family at these get-togethers than we did at home. I enjoyed sitting near the adult men and listening to them talk. I also enjoyed sitting on the floor in the den while listening to the women talk in the kitchen. If you wanted to know what was going on, all you had to do was be invisible and listen.

No one was dirt poor, and no one was financially well off. There really wasn't a spiritually impoverished person there either. Much of our individual security came from the knowledge that each family was part of a much larger one. We each knew that if something happened, there would be more than just one person available and willing to help.

And things did happen. One of the nineteen cousins contracted polio. Everyone was heartbroken, and Grammy got physically and emotionally involved. This group of people was afraid of very little.

Three of the sons or sons-in-law served in the Second World War, with the fourth being rejected because of eyesight. He was really disappointed because he couldn't serve. Their serving not only made you proud of them but made you feel as though you were connected to America.

Some were union members; others were not, but there was no animosity. There were cigarette and pipe smokers outside and always away from the kids and the food. No booze was served in the house, though there might have been a small bottle or two in one of the cars. After dessert, some of the uncles enjoyed their cigarettes, and maybe even a toddy, while leaning on one of the cars in the driveway.

We were not all of the same religious faith, but we enjoyed a prayer before each meal and a few hymns in the living room before we went home. Group pictures were always taken, usually in the front of the house, before the sun set and anyone left. Every family brought a camera and used it sparingly.

In addition to the family reunions, my grandparents visited our house one evening a week to play games. They'd bring ice cream. As years passed, we eventually purchased a television and Grandpa loved to watch the episodes of *Life of Riley* starring William Bendix.

Weekday evenings when my dad was at work, I often visited Grandpa and played checkers with him. He had a bad shoulder from falling off my aunt and uncle's roof when he had helped them build their home. While we were playing checkers, he kept a heating pad on it to stop the pain. If I lost a certain number of games, I had to memorize verses from the Bible. For years, he was much better at checkers than I; therefore, I learned a lot of verses.

On some summer nights, our next-door neighbor's son Stan, who was nicer to us than his brother Luke, took Julie and me to the outdoor movies. He had a flatbed truck and we stood in the back and watched the movie while he and his girlfriend sat real close in the front seat. No funny stuff.

His truck was large, so he had to park it in the back row, but we didn't care. Our favorite part of the evening was intermission when we got to have something inexpensive to eat and drink.

Late on Friday nights, the Gillette fights were on television, and occasionally Luke let me come over to his house and watch the fights through the living room window. He never invited me inside though. I stood on a box outside the window and watched the fights while he entertained his girlfriend on the couch. He teased and tickled her all during the fights. I heard her screams and the television volume through the screen door. The fights were exciting and much more educational than what they were doing on the couch.

During the month of October, we'd take our annual trip to the mountains. The entire clan would head up to a favorite park in the Presidential Range where we picnicked and then played games or walked the park. It was always cool and beautiful.

I'll never forget one October trip when Grammy quietly took out her false teeth and began eating pickled pig's feet. If you want to see a person age right before your eyes, watch them do that. I was amazed! I realized she and Grandpa had to take their false teeth out at night and put them in a glass of water while they slept, but I had never seen my beautiful grandmother eat without her teeth.

CHAPTER 18

The Big Move

Relocating usually refers to moving your family from one location to another. The first move I remember is when we moved from my grandparents' house to our home. The move was exciting for the whole family.

Each home seemed to have a different smell, feel, and level of social activity. My grandmother's house had a wonderful food smell and was busy with people going in and out all of the time. As time passed, our new home felt warm and comfortable and had the smell of my mother's cooking. It felt like a home should feel—a safe sanctuary.

Guptill Elementary School felt safe. I knew every day, as I looked out the school window, that I'd be walking the same roads home after the last school bell rang and seeing the same classmates the next day, and that recess would be filled with the same fun games and competitors. It was intellectually challenging and, at the same time, comfortably predictable.

I remember my last day of grammar school. The teacher asked each class member to stand up and tell the class what he or she thought of their grammar school experience and then share their plans for the summer.

Country kids like me had limited plans for the summer: stay out of trouble, stay out of sight, and enjoy the wonderful freedom of no school and no homework. Some got up and talked about taking trips with their folks, going to camp, or going to the ocean. I was jealous and had listened to enough. So when it came to my turn, I told the class that my dad was taking me to France to meet our relatives there. We were going to spend his vacation week meeting distant relatives we'd never seen before. We also planned to visit some of the historic places in Paris.

The class and the teacher were impressed, and I left grammar school with a puffed-up chest and a wide smile. A couple of nights later, my dad woke me up when he got home from work and asked me about the trip. "It was all over town. I heard about it at the mill. Why did you do that, Jacob?"

I had embarrassed him again. I told him I was sorry, but personally I didn't regret the performance. Revenge was sweet. I found out later that the cost of my dad's loss of confidence and trust in me was not a good price to pay. The Bible says that revenge is the Lord's, not ours. I, like many others, had to learn that the hard way.

—⁂—

A promotion to junior high school predestined relocation. The step up to the seventh grade meant attending a new school across town with new teachers and a lot of unknowns. I dwelt a lot on the disadvantages of the relocation and couldn't find many good things to think about. My sister had made the move a year before and didn't like it that much.

Our junior high was housed in the same building as the high school, which made the relocation a significant change in social activity and was much more preadult oriented. The school building was a half mile further from home and involved a bus ride. The bus came quite early in the morning, and I realized on my first few rides that I missed the exercise, the sun, and changing weather; but most of all, I missed the closeness of the trees and deep woods. There was very little adventure in riding the bus.

I liked meeting new kids from other parts of the city, but this meant lots more academic competition for top grades. For some reason, Mrs. Champion, my sixth-grade teacher, had felt I had significant potential and made sure that I was placed in an advanced junior high class. I was complimented and amazed. She had good intentions, but I wasn't as confident of my potential as she was.

This change was not about physical work, which I loved and knew I could do as well as anyone, but it was about improved listening, studying more in the evenings, memorizing more facts, and being able to describe clearly and concisely what I had learned. All of the above were not my strengths. I felt I had fooled them for six years; now I'd be out in the open competing with all of the kids my age in the city, and I wasn't prepared. My self-confidence was obviously not where it needed to be.

I kept thinking that there must be a good side to this. The Scriptures taught me to look up and live one day at a time. More important, they taught me that I was not alone and that Christ would never leave me. I also surmised that everyone else who passed this way faced the same challenges and most likely had similar fears.

On the good side, joining junior high school made me feel I was becoming part of something much bigger than our local neighborhood. I experienced a similar feeling in the winter when I shoveled snow for customers across town, not just on local streets where I knew everyone. That thought was invigorating, and I kept it in mind as I rode the bus those first few weeks of school.

—∙∙∙—

This relocation was a big deal and changed me more than I imagined it would. It wasn't all about school though. There were new activities that kept me balanced during this time, but it took me the entire two years of junior high to put the protective security of attending Guptill Elementary School behind me. I guess that is why they call it junior high school. It helps you prepare for the last big four years.

Little League baseball was the first new activity and adventure I became involved in. The drafting process for team selections took place on the baseball diamond at the "Common" on Main Street.

Buck Jones, the guy in grammar school who wanted to beat the tar out of me after school, was a pitcher on another team. I truly enjoyed his pitching success. He was a good fastball pitcher. As I stood at the plate, I wondered if he really wanted to hit me with the ball (some of his pitches came very close). We never talked much, but I did my best to hit his pitches out of the park. I never did, but I did hit a lot of doubles off his fastball.

Grandpa loved baseball but never attended any of my games. However, Pepére, who loved to boat and fish and had little interest in baseball, attended many of my games. He surprised and pleased me by being there and also by sometimes bringing my mom with my little four-year-old sister and two-year-old brother in tow. We had no car, so Pepére reached out to his daughter-in-law and did the right thing. I had been taught that the word *love* as a verb means that it is what you do and not what you say that proves you love them.

Baseball doesn't let young boys daydream. It makes them stay awake even when things are boring and slow. Sounds like what a good student has to learn. Young boys have to learn to sacrifice when the coach signals to do so. Amazingly, it's learning to do your part no matter what the cost is, and that the team's successes are more important than individual successes. These and many other lessons were learned, all helping me adjust to junior high school.

The two years that I played Little League baseball were positive ones for me. I batted in the top five, our team won the city championship, and I reveled in the physical contact and intensity of the catcher's position.

—◊◊◊—

The second activity was related to travel and transportation. Earlier, my parents had purchased two J. C. Higgins bikes, one for my sister and one for me. Her bike was green and white, and mine was red and white. They each had springs on the front to absorb the shock of bumps.

Julie and I learned to ride well, so much so that I could stand on my seat with no hands on the handlebar while going downhill. One day, however, while biking down Adams Avenue, she tried it. She was wearing her new, white dress that my mother had made her. Julie quickly went off the road, down the hill, through the woods, and into a swamp. I ran down and pulled her and her bike out of the mud. She wasn't hurt, but her whole body was covered with creek mud, leaves, and other stuff. I then walked her back to my grandmother's with her crying all of the way. I felt bad until I got chewed out for her lack of bike-riding skills.

Bussing was fine for some, but for me it was like riding to school in a sardine can. We only lived a couple of miles away. My parents gave Julie and me a choice, and I chose to ride my bike, with or without my sister. For me, biking was going to make going to junior high school more acceptable. And, no, I wouldn't melt on rainy days. My sister announced that there would be no biking for her to and from school. She was riding the bus. I guess she needed more social contact. I think she liked a guy who rode on the bus. Whatever her reason was, I was now free to ride the roads of my choosing back and forth to school. At last, I had the privacy and freedom I loved.

—⁓—

A third series of events helped in my transition to junior high school. My mother and I began a project to upgrade our backyard. New Hampshire soil is beautifully dark and can grow almost anything. It was perfect for growing witch grass and other weeds. Mom wanted a rock flower garden, maple trees, and a beautiful lawn.

The project was larger in size than any I had been involved in before and required more of me physically. My primary challenge was to turn the soil over with a shovel, pull out all of the weeds, rake it flat, seed it, and water it. After that, I could plant the trees and build the rock flower garden.

Some of the raked excess loam became the base of the elevated flower garden. This was serious work and Mom helped with the weeding. It was a tough project, but for weeks we both looked forward to working it every morning. It seemed as though she was always working, and because I felt that I had lost some of her respect when as a young kid I had stolen some cookies, I continually worked hard to regain it.

While working together on the backyard project, she mentioned that she may need to go to work in the future, but told me that Dad had more than once said no to her working. Mom was a subtle person much of the time, and I was learning that she was not as content as she appeared to be. Or maybe I had been asleep and was just waking up. Her comment about needing to go to work reminded me of the evening years before when I had seen her in her bedroom leaning over her cedar chest moving baby clothes around. I wondered what was going on and asked, "We aren't going to have more babies are we?"

Mom never looked up. She just replied, "You had better ask your dad."

It was Saturday, so he was sitting in the den reading the paper and smoking his pipe. I asked him the same question and followed it with, "Dad you know we're broke most of the time and can't afford any more kids."

He dropped his paper and knocked me flat on my butt with his open hand and said, "Don't you ever talk to me about that again. It is none of your business."

I got the message. He felt I was being insolent, and I felt that Mom had set me up. She was pregnant with their third child, my younger sister, Jackie. Two years and four months later, my brother, Monty, was born.

Now with four kids and no car, Mom had been confined to home for years. Her sisters' and brother's families had cars, which I'm sure she noticed and envied. Her closest and younger sister, Beverly, with whom she shared almost everything, had children, a good job at the phone company, was involved in community and church activities, and had a husband who, much like Dad, had served in the military and could be described as a tough disciplinarian at home. One difference, however, was his willingness to let my aunt work outside the home.

I learned in school that when my dad returned from the South Pacific he could have gone back to school and finished his education on the G.I. Bill. Without more education, it was hard for him to materially improve our household income, and I asked him about it. He talked about the program but really wasn't interested in going back to school. Dad seemed to be content with life, but I could tell Mom wasn't.

My parents' bedroom was across the hall from mine. Some of their conversations at night drove me nuts. Many times, I knocked on their bedroom door and asked if everything was all right. My dad did not like the interruptions and, of course, let me know it.

My ten-year-younger brother and I shared a bedroom. He was lots of fun, but we both needed some privacy. I encouraged my parents to let me move upstairs into the unfinished attic. The truth was that trouble was brewing in River City. I felt that eventually Dad and I were going to get into it if I stayed on the first floor. Better that I move upstairs.

—⁂—

Talk about product dissatisfaction. I was not happy at all with my J. C. Higgins bike. It was my primary transportation and I had issues which included lack of speed, loose front end with the shock absorption spring, inability to gear down on hills, and general lack of safe performance when going wide open down steep hills. I'd outgrown my bike.

Since the bike had been a gift from my parents, I had to be careful. I looked around and found that there were a lot of different bikes, many of them foreign made. That was not good news, considering the postwar feelings about foreign products. Western Auto had a number of bikes, as did a bike shop near school, but I knew I couldn't afford to trade up. My parents had stretched to buy me the bike I had. If I was going to upgrade, I'd have to find my own way to do it.

Rick Carver and I became friends while playing Little League baseball together. He came from another grammar school across town and was making the relocation adjustment to junior high school just as I was. Rick needed a bike to ride to and from school and couldn't afford one. He liked mine. His dad kept a lot of metal junk piled up in his backyard. One day, I noticed a Hercules bike frame there. The frame had no wheels, handlebar, seat, or fenders. It was just a frame with a sprocket. It was going to be sold for the value of its metal content. We pulled it out of the tall grass and pile of junk and cleaned it up a bit. Rick asked his dad if he could have it and he said, "Sure."

Rick and I talked. The good news was he really wanted my bike. I had kept it in excellent condition, had added a light and horn to the handlebar, and put a rack for my school books over the rear fender.

I told Rick I was seriously interested in the Hercules frame and asked him if he could come up with some money so that we could make a trade. He went into the house and came out with five dollars, which he said was all he had. I knew that five dollars would buy a lot of parts that this junk needed. You've heard the saying, money talks and everything else walks—it's true.

I handed him my bike, pocketed the five dollars, lifted the Hercules frame to my shoulder, and headed home. Rick ran back into the house excited about his new bike. He was satisfied and so was I. He had helped me discover the bike of my dreams. I couldn't believe it.

As I walked home, I kept trying to convince myself that it was easy, but I must have stopped twenty times to rest. The bike frame was clumsy and my shoulders didn't like the thin frame.

Though thinner and lighter than my J. C. Higgins, the frame was stable and had high-speed potential. I had a few bucks, plus the five dollars from Rick, and knew I could earn a lot more. I cleaned the frame with soap and water and then polished it with some car polish that Pepére had left on a shelf in the garage. The few scratches didn't show much after the cleaning and polishing. It was just a matter of time and work before my dream would become a reality.

During the negotiations with Rick, I thought about my parents and concluded that they wouldn't approve of the trade. Hercules was a racing bike and the company sponsored many successful bike riders in Europe. The Hercules frame was made in England and since they were allies during the war, I figured Dad wouldn't have a problem with the manufacturer. But I knew I would disappoint them, considering the J. C. Higgins was their gift to me. Nevertheless, I decided I knew more about bikes and my needs than they did and felt they'd eventually get past it. I knew I'd pay a price in the short run, but I was learning that in the real world, nothing is free.

My mom was disappointed with my trade and my dad said, "You made your bed, now lie in it." I'd say they didn't share my vision. A generation gap was building, and I felt in my bones that this wasn't the last time I'd significantly disappoint them.

I approached my grandmother for work. She surprised me when she shared that she was so pleased with my mom's new rock flower garden that she wanted me to build her one. She said she always wanted a rock flower garden, but no one had the time to make it.

Years before, my uncle used his trailer to deliver rocks to both Grammy's house and our house. The rocks came from his wooded lot. Mom had requested round white rocks; Grammy wanted flat ones. I had used the white rocks for Mom's rock flower garden and the flat ones were still lying under the trees in Grammy's backyard.

I was learning that timing is everything. When I started building the stone wall for Grammy's garden, Grandpa came out and in a know-it-all fashion stated, "You can't make a wall without stakes, a line, and some sighting."

Quietly but insistently, Grammy responded, "Help or go find something else to do." What a tigress!

She loved the garden when it was finished and, as time passed, spent hours in it nurturing and tending her flowers. After finishing the garden, I cleaned the chicken house. The last project she had for me to do was stacking wood in the house shed.

With Grammy's projects completed, I moved down the street and washed the kitchen walls and ceiling for a French lady. She recommended me to the wife of the hardware store owner; I washed her walls and ceilings. And on and on it went.

Two months later, I had a 3-speed Hercules bike that had new thin wheels; tires; brakes; seat; thin, small fenders; classic mud flaps; bright reflectors; rear spring-loaded carrier; and perfect handlebar and grips. My new chrome light and horn glistened in the sunlight. I had kept my old lock, chain, and key.

I biked up Rochester hill, turned around, and raced back down the hill to Franklin Street. At top speed, I kept up with the traffic. It ran like a dream. My skin tingled all over—I felt truly blessed and thought, *God is so good!*

I was gaining more confidence, and the relocation to junior high school was getting easier by the month.

Enjoying team sports

CHAPTER 19

Winter's Joy

Winter in New Hampshire was a special time of the year, especially for young kids looking for something physically challenging to do. It seemed that many of our winter snowstorms left us with lots of the white stuff. When the snow was two feet deep, everyone lived in the same generation.

After each snowstorm, I had a work role to play for the family. My task was to shovel a path from the house to the garage, where we stored chicken pellets and crushed shells for the chickens, and from the garage to the chicken house. I was also responsible for shoveling under the clothesline and digging a path from the back door and down the driveway to the mailbox.

As storms came and went, I came to love shoveling snow. It was invigorating, especially early in the morning before the sun came up. After the storm passed, the sky was crystal blue and the perfectly white snow glistened and shined like polished chrome.

Nobody complained, not even the chickens, when I got up early and started shoveling my first path to the garage and chicken house. The chicken house was usually warm and dry. Most of the eggs were still warm, and the chickens were always ready to eat. When I entered, the old rooster pranced around making all kinds of noise until I dropped the pellets and some crushed shells into the feeder. Then you could hear a pin drop. The crushed shells were added to their feed to provide calcium, which when digested made the eggshells harder.

The paths to the garage and chicken house were on grass, so the snow was easy to remove. The shovel I liked most was a grain shovel like those used at the feed store to move grain around. It was aluminum and could hold a large load. When the edge of the shovel became dull, I sharpen it with a file. The coal shovel was good on ice because it was square, smaller but heavier, and made of steel. It could also be sharpened with a file. I was beginning to realize that excellent tools made work so much more fun. Both shovels were needed around our house, as well as several others.

Since we didn't have a car yet, shoveling the long driveway could be completed anytime, as long as it was done before dark. Some snowdrifts were huge. Most storms whipped the snow around the house and created two drifts near the back porch, right where my path to the garage had to be dug.

When we had big storms, the snowplows ran around-the-clock, so keeping the end of the driveway clean was an off-and-on project, which was fine with me. Whenever those storms occurred, I waited with hope and anticipation for the school-closing announcements. A no-school day was a gift to be cherished.

—⁂—

I cut a deal with my mom. As long as all of the paths were shoveled and I promised to finish the driveway before dark, I could walk our side of town looking for driveways to shovel. I usually got up early and had the paths done before seven o'clock. I then grabbed some pocket food and headed down the road.

It was an adventure every time. Adams Avenue was my first target, more than a half mile away. There were three driveways that usually needed shoveling. If the snowplows had gone through and piled lots of snow and ice in front of the mailboxes, I first cleared that snow away so that mail could be delivered.

I shoveled my grandparents' driveway first. Theirs was my top priority as Grammy sometimes came home for lunch or only worked half a day.

Next, I went to the O'Neals', who had the longest driveway. Their house had a rear garage, so the driveway was L-shaped. Mr. O'Neal also paid the most. He never paid me less than five dollars and almost always included a tip. His two kids would be looking out the window making faces and having fun. Mrs. O'Neal taught school, so she was home when school was out and always offered me something to eat and drink.

My third customer on Adams Avenue was a retired French lady who took care of her mother. I made sure that her driveway was immaculate and removed all of the snow from her car and front porch. During the spring and fall, she paid me to wash her painted plaster walls and ceilings.

After those three customers, I continued walking until I found someone else to help. It was a very successful day when I came home with twenty dollars net of lunch and other refreshment expenses. The average income in America at that time was ninety dollars per week or eighteen dollars per day, and the minimum wage was seventy-five cents per hour; so I felt I had done very well.

Part of the joy of shoveling snow on the road was stopping in a small grocery store on Portland Street and buying the kind of junk food I never got at home or at school. Sometimes, I bought a large Moxie drink and a dozen sugared doughnuts.

One afternoon while I was away shoveling, my dad put the rubbish cans on top of the snowbank at the end of the driveway before he went to work, and he left a message for me to put them away after the rubbish truck came by.

I headed home in the middle of the afternoon so that I could finish our driveway before four o'clock when it got dark. When I finished shoveling the driveway, I moved the cans, which were still full, to the end of the driveway near the road for the trash collectors to empty when they came by. I figured I'd hear the truck, so I thought nothing more about it.

It had snowed some during the day while I was away, so I cleaned up the paths and shoveled under the clothesline. And then I went in for supper. The evening passed quickly and I headed to the attic to go to bed. I loved sleeping there—it was my sanctuary.

The attic had two windows providing light and a great view. The walls were just wood shingles nailed to slats, so you could hear birds, traffic, and anything that went on outside. As the morning sun rose on the east side of the house, rays of sunlight filtered through some of the shingles. The floor was rough wood and wasn't nailed down. There was insulation under those loose floorboards, but none on the walls and ceiling. That was great in summer because it kept it cool at night, but not great in the winter.

I had a wooden desk with one drawer and an old dresser that once belonged to my French grandmother who died of cancer at age forty-eight. Somehow the dresser ended up in the attic when I needed it. I also had an old brass bed, and my mother and grandmother made quilts so that I'd be warm on unusually cold nights. I was never cold when I buried myself under the quilts. The problem was, however, that once under the quilts I heard very little.

Deep asleep, as usual, at a quarter past ten I was awakened by the sound of my dad tripping over the trash cans as he turned into the driveway. He usually ran the half-mile home from Portland Street where his work buddy dropped him off.

"Oh, no," I said to myself and really hoped he wasn't hurt. I ran downstairs and out the back door. He was coming up the driveway holding on to his shoulder. I couldn't believe it! I'd forgotten and left the trash cans out after he specifically instructed me to put them away.

I apologized over and over again. Dad said nothing. When times were tough or when he was injured, he never said much. He just hunkered down and got through it. I really liked that about him and wanted to be like that whenever I got hurt or in trouble. No noise, just gut it out.

His shoulder was seriously damaged, and it took a long time to heal; but he never complained. And I never again forgot any assignment he gave to me. Dad and God forgave me for my stupidity long before I forgave myself. Christ took away my guilt after lots of prayer, and after I developed a renewed focus on my responsibilities.

—w—

Late at night, it seemed to be a long way from my bed to the bathroom downstairs, and during the winter it was a cold walk as well. So, one cold night when I really had to go, I looked over to the back window and thought to myself, *Why not?* No one would know the difference, and the grass might appreciate the fertilizer. The window opened easily, but the screen only went up four to five inches, so I had to pee very carefully out the window. I pulled the half-stuck screen down quietly and closed the window. This was great, my own urinal.

The next day was Sunday, and we were all sitting at breakfast together. All of the shoveling had been completed the day before; Mom had completed her Saturday washing, and we were talking about getting ready to head for Sunday school and church.

Dad asked me, "How did you sleep last night?"

"Fine," I replied.

"Did you have to get up during the night?"

"Yes, just to go to the bathroom."

He smiled and I knew I was in trouble. He asked, "Did you feed the chickens this morning?"

"Yes I did, around seven o'clock."

Something was up! Dad wasn't this interested in my morning activities. In fact, we were allowed to stay up Friday nights and wait for him to come home from work. Many times I asked him, "What are we going to do tomorrow?" He always responded, "Jacob, let tomorrow take care of itself," but I never did like that answer. I liked planning the next day and then managing every detail of it.

Dad's questions continued. "Did you notice anything unusual on the way to and from the chicken house?"

"No I didn't," I said.

"Come with me!" he instructed.

While walking through the kitchen, Dad asked in a low voice, "Have you ever taken a leak through the attic window?"

I automatically responded, "Of course not. I'd never do that."

We walked outside and he looked towards the clotheslines under my attic window. It was beautiful. There were dozens of small, yellow icicles hanging from the window and shingles below the window. There were also large, yellow icicles on the sheets my mother had left hanging on the clotheslines overnight.

My dad couldn't stop laughing. I looked back at the door we came through; Mom and Julie were standing there, also caught up in laughter.

I was humbled. *Why do I respond so quickly and thoughtlessly with a lie?*, I wondered. *What drives me to do such stupid things? Lord, help me stop being such a liar and fool, please!*

When Dad stopped laughing, he said, "Jacob, I think you really need to go to church today!" I knew inside what he meant, and he was right. Only God could solve my problem.

CHAPTER 20

Grammy's Touch

Grammy was the family's quiet leader. If she ever made a loud noise, it was wonderful rolling laughter, or it was somebody's name being called. Loud for Grammy was close to normal for most of the other adults in her family.

She was only about five feet three inches tall and when standing by Grandpa, who was six feet four, appeared even shorter. But when she was at the kitchen or dining room table seated on her special cushion, she was almost as tall as the tallest.

In her late teens and early twenties, Grammy was rather sickly. This delayed her marriage to Grandpa. She was really thin when they married, but over the years, like most, she gained a few pounds.

She never cut her hair. So it was quite long, but you wouldn't know it because it was thin and always braided, with the braids neatly pinned up in a circular fashion around her head. One of her granddaughters followed her example by never cutting her hair and wearing it braided.

For years, Grammy worked in the finishing room at the woolen mill in a neighboring town. She, with others, repaired imperfections in the bolts of wool fabrics before they were shipped to customers.

I visited her many times at work and was amazed at how fast her hands and fingers moved with needles and repair tools accomplishing her mission. This would seem normal, except for the fact that she suffered with the pain of arthritis in her hands and fingers. The swollen joints even prevented her from fully opening up the palms of her hands. Halfway was about all she could manage. Nevertheless, she accomplished much without complaint. She was a great example to all of us.

Grammy spent hours at her sewing machine making all kinds of clothes for the family. Some of my favorite shirts, and ones that kept me the warmest in the winter, were the lined, wool, button-down shirts she made for me. She made clothes all year long and at Christmas gave them to us as gifts. There were no favorites; everyone got gifts of equal value.

She enjoyed going to church and attended the ladies' Sunday school class, which was held in the choir loft. (Before spending monies on expansion, growing churches in those days used every available space.) Grammy always kept her Bible near-at-hand. She underlined passages and treated her Bible as a reference guide and notebook. I watched as she lived out her religious beliefs, but I never saw or heard her push her beliefs on anyone. She tried to help everyone; those she couldn't help, she prayed for.

With one of her delicate handkerchiefs, she'd wipe her nose and then tuck the handkerchief in her bra. It never showed, but we all knew it was there. When she hugged and gave you a kiss, she always smelled good. I don't think it was perfume. She just had a wonderful, unique scent.

Grammy always wore a dress, many of which she made herself. Once she put her apron on over her dress, she was in her work clothes. It hadn't become fashionable yet for ladies to wear slacks, not even those working in the factories and mills.

I loved to watch her make lye soap in the basement wash area. Grammy usually made it in the fall after the pigs had been butchered and pork fat was available. Grandpa made lots of wooden boxes for her to fill with the lye mixture. Once filled, she left the boxes on the basement floor until the mixture was dried and cured. Then, using her black butcher knife, she cut the soap into squares and stacked them on shelves under the basement stairs. Her fingers must have hurt terribly when she cut the hard soap. Again, she never complained. The soap was used to wash clothes and just about everything else.

It seemed that Grammy was always busy working on something, except when she took a little nap. The only thing she complained about was the fact that she sometimes had trouble sleeping at night. I noticed she often dozed off for a short while in the evenings as she sat in her den chair knitting or sewing something. She had the right to. Except for Sundays, she got up at five-thirty every morning. I once asked her if she felt that the naps might account for her sleeplessness at night. Her response was, "What naps?" I think she meant it.

—⁂—

Early in their marriage, Grandpa occasionally smoked cigars. At the same time, he was a deacon in the church. Grammy pointed out to him many times that his smoking was not setting a good example for his family or others in the church. He'd say, "I only smoke at home and everyone knows a man's home is his castle."

One day while he was smoking his cigar in the den, the church pastor came to visit. Grammy happened to be sitting on the front porch getting some sun. The pastor got out of his car and walked up to the porch. He talked with Grammy for a while. Grandpa hadn't heard the car or any of the conversation. When Grammy led the pastor into the smoked-filled den, Grandpa was totally embarrassed. He apologized for the smoke and walked directly into the kitchen, put the cigar out, and tossed it into the stove. After the pastor left, he walked back into the kitchen and told Grammy he'd never smoke again—and he never did.

Grammy never shared, and I believe never learned, what was said in the den between Grandpa and the pastor. I often wondered if Grammy set Grandpa up. She was very smart, but not devious. I knew personally that she was a lioness. If she did set him up, it was for the right reason, and I believe she got away with it. But that's just one admirer's perspective.

—⁂—

Grammy organized most of our family reunions. Whether they were held inside or out depended entirely upon the weather. Summer reunions were usually held outdoors in their backyard where enough picnic tables were set up to hold all the food plus seat everyone.

At one reunion, after everyone had eaten and the tables had been cleared off, I watched Grandpa and Grammy fall asleep on a lawn blanket.

They each started snoring, so we kids gathered around to listen. It wasn't music and it wasn't loud, but it was unique. Their snores sounded as if they were motoring up gentle hills. They'd stop for a few seconds and coast back down. When they interrupted their trip with funny sounds, we all laughed. Our laughter eventually woke them up and they shooed us away.

Grandpa liked to tease, especially the girls. He also liked practical jokes. Grammy was the opposite. She focused on doing: getting things done, quietly lining up the next project, or writing a note of encouragement to someone. She focused on touching someone in need, and for that she will never leave my heart.

CHAPTER 21

Uncle Larry's Place

The country road weaved between dairy farms and paralleled the
Salmon Falls River. The grass on the side of the road was three feet
tall, making the road look narrower than it really was. Distant grazing
cows could barely be seen in the fields of tall grass. The hills and valleys
were lush and dark green from the recent spring rains; the river was full
and even overflowing in some places. The beauty of the New England
countryside on the way to Uncle Larry's farm was unique.

Uncle Larry, being one of Grammy's brothers, was my great-uncle. He
lived in southeast Maine, about twenty-five miles from our home in New
Hampshire. Much like Grammy, he had a warm and likeable personality.
He didn't talk a lot, but when you did chat with him he was very friendly
and open. He had a great smile that he readily shared with others.

Uncle Larry seemed to enjoy being with the family. At family get-
togethers, he drove up in his large, dark-green Ford flatbed truck, which
he kept absolutely immaculate. The finish on the flatbed part resembled
new wood. He kept his carpenter tools locked behind the cab of the truck
in the large, wooden toolbox bolted to the truck's bed.

He often visited Grammy, and on each visit brought vegetables, fruit,
frozen meat, and/or wood for winter. Seeing how much stuff he brought,
I naturally imagined that he owned and managed a large farm with lots
of helpers. But I was wrong. He lived alone; and the items he shared with

the family had been personally planted, weeded, harvested, frozen, or with regard to the wood, cut and chopped by him.

The summer I turned twelve, Uncle Larry invited me to stay and work with him on his farm; so with my parents' blessings, I did. I'm sure that at twelve, I was really more than my mom wanted to handle all summer long. As she was already quite busy with my younger sister and brother, my leaving for a while would make things a little easier for her. It was agreed that I could stay for a week. This was such a big deal to me. I could barely believe that I was going—and for a whole week!

To put this into perspective, earlier that spring I read about Edmund Hillary and Tenzing Norgay climbing Mount Everest on May 19th. They were the first to climb the 29,035 foot mountain, and it was an amazing feat. The invitation to stay at the farm and work with Uncle Larry every day was as big a deal to me personally as the climb was to them. I wasn't going to screw it up!

Grammy dropped me off at Uncle Larry's, and he agreed to drive me home a week later. I tried not to show my excitement too much when I first arrived, but I'm sure he could see it.

I was immediately impressed by what I saw. I had visited many other farms but none like his. The neatness was inspiring. Everything had a place and nothing was out of place. I thought it was the kind of farm Christ would have owned and worked had he been a farmer as well as a carpenter.

His farm was small, not large as I imagined it to be. The two-story farmhouse had a front porch, much like our porch at home. It faced the road, was open and completely shaded by overhanging branches from the huge, tall maple tree at the front corner of the house. We ended up spending most of our evenings sitting out there enjoying the shade and cool breeze while we relaxed and ate dessert. On the back side of the house, a breezeway (or open passage), connected the house to the barn.

His long, gravel driveway ran past the house and barn, through an open field, and then into the woods. Across from the farmhouse, and on the other side of the driveway, was his garage and workshop. Behind the garage was a smaller building once used to house chickens, and behind that building was an empty pigpen. Like us, he'd long before given up on pigs, and I assumed he didn't keep chickens anymore because Grammy did. Why take care of chickens when he could trade for eggs?

Uncle Larry put my stuff in the large upstairs bedroom. The bedroom had eight-inch wooden floorboards that were painted battleship gray. Everything in the bedroom was spotless. There were two military cots for sleeping, a night table, a lamp, and a dresser. The closet door was open; I saw his military uniform hanging on the back side of the door, as if ready to be worn in a parade. I stacked my stuff in a corner of the bedroom.

As I left the room, I noticed the windows were open a couple of inches, just enough to let fresh air in but not rain. The window shades were pulled halfway down to keep the sun's heat and rays at bay. I said to myself, *This guy has got it together.* I was excited and really looking forward to the week.

Each morning at the crack of dawn, we were summoned to rise and shine by the musical chirping of the birds outside our open windows. Up we'd get and head downstairs to wash up and get ready for the daily chores. The radio was turned on the moment Uncle Larry's feet hit the first floor. Listening to farm reports and country music was new to me. I rather enjoyed the change.

I washed up using the small washbasin on the counter just off the kitchen. Uncle Larry washed and shaved in the metal kitchen sink. He scrubbed himself so hard with Lava soap that his skin was red. Some might say he was obsessively clean and neat; I just wanted to be like him. The smell of Lava soap became my close companion.

Work had to be done before we ate. We began by feeding the cows and heifers some grain and hay. Then we milked. The cow-milking experience caused the most laughter during my visit. My intensity worked against me as I tried to pull and squeeze a teat at the same time. The cow kept turning her head to watch as I fumbled around. In the middle of his laughter, Uncle Larry encouraged me to focus on other chores.

Then we took the fresh, raw milk into the house and ran it through a separator, which was in a workroom next to the kitchen. After the milk and cream were separated, he placed multiple containers of each in a small refrigerator. This room was really a huge walk-in pantry with windows. It had lots of shelves full of cooking utensils and dry food products like sugar, flour, and spices. On wash day it became the laundry room. Using his wringer-type washing machine, he'd run the washed wet clothes through the wringers, which squeezed out the water, before he hung the clothes out on the line to dry.

After washing the separator and utensils, we rinsed them with boiling hot water. We then washed ourselves up again, and he prepared breakfast. Uncle Larry was thin and not very tall, so I had assumed he wasn't a big eater. The good news was that I was wrong. We had eggs, bacon, fruit, and toast with Grammy's homemade jam on it. He had coffee and I had milk. The jam was one of the items he traded for when he visited Grammy. We both had two servings of everything, and I decided I was moving to the farm full-time. We cleaned the dishes and pans and again rinsed everything with boiling hot water.

Uncle Larry put some milk in a bowl for the barn cats. Not having seen them yet, I asked him where they were. He told me they weren't too friendly and spent most of their time catching mice, which was fine with him. By then, the cows and heifers had finished their grain and hay and were ready to be led out to pasture. We cleaned the stalls and washed them down with a hose. The barn smelled great again.

Now it was time for me to use the john. The outhouse, which was inside the barn, was in the back past the cow stalls. The small room appeared to have been added to the barn years ago. The walls, ceiling, and floor were clean and made of finished wood. It didn't take too long for me to realize that I didn't have to look down the hole every time I used the room—nothing down there changed.

Why two seats?, I wondered. Do people actually go to the bathroom together? I never asked Uncle Larry and still don't know the answer. Everything was clean and neat, and the smell of the hay from the barn made being there both relieving and tolerable.

It seemed as though I was always opening or closing gates on the farm. There were so many. Some were all metal, some were all wood, and some were a combination of wood and metal. Each set of gate hinges was as unique as the gates themselves. With all of those differences, I assumed that they were built during different time periods and maybe by different people.

I found that some of the gates just provided a passageway through the moss-covered stone walls, while others were between the end of a stone wall and a building. I couldn't imagine how long it took to build all those walls. The stones were rough and jagged—different from those in my part of New Hampshire. I did notice that the stones were stacked much neater than those in the wall behind my home, and the thought occurred to me that restacking the stones in our wall would be an interesting project for me to do someday—maybe.

I did see two of the cats during the week. One was almost friendly, so I tried to pet her. She stuck around for a few minutes and then took off into the barn. The tomcat had no interest in getting to know me. I tried to corner him in the hay; he hissed and jumped for a cross beam and then headed for God knows where. One morning, I saw him with a mouse in his mouth. He wasn't interested in sharing and quickly scooted under the barn with it.

Mutt, Uncle Larry's long-eared and short-legged basset hound followed us everywhere. He was a hunter and constantly sniffing everything. Mutt was a very friendly dog and I enjoyed having him around.

After I had asked him numerous questions, Uncle Larry shared a few things about himself with me. He'd been released from military service because of a heart condition and warned not to marry. He was told that if he did marry, too much stress would be put on his heart and result in death. Uncle Larry received no disability checks because the military said his heart problem was there before he entered the service. Now he worked as a full-time carpenter and part-time farmer. He was proud to have been in the army and missed it, and he still wore some of his army clothes. I more than liked Uncle Larry, I respected him.

The great news for me was that there was always something meaningful to do there. We spent much of the time cutting down trees, then removing the limbs, and dragging the logs up to the farm. This was the first step in getting firewood ready for the winter. Using his two-man crosscut saw, we worked well together as we sawed each log slowly, cutting it into approximately two-and-a-half-foot lengths. Then we stacked them for splitting later, after the wood had dried. We took our time; I watched him closely, looking for signs of stress. His heart condition paced our work, which made it enjoyable and still productive.

Uncle Larry not only had a tractor but lots of other farm equipment as well. The tractor was an old Chevrolet with the body of the car removed, except for the dash, hood, and radiator. The seat was a small, homemade, padded bench; the rear frame had been shortened just enough to accommodate a duel rear end and wheels.

It was great to ride on the tractor, and he let me drive it most of the time. He'd ask if I wanted to go for a drive and, without hesitation, I always said yes. We drove on the old dirt road in front of his house, but most of our rides were on roads in the woods and along stone walls where white birch trees and berry bushes covered them. Every trip was a new adventure.

The most fun for me was driving the tractor through the woods and fields. We bounced along, dragging two or more logs and sucking up the warm air, cool shade, and sunshine. When we were thirsty, we shared the cold jar of iced tea wrapped in a grain sack on the floor of the tractor. I tried not to jerk the gas pedal as we went over bumps, but I wasn't very successful. Uncle Larry just smiled and looked the other way.

One of our trips took us down the road a short distance to where he grew up. The original homestead no longer belonged to the family, but the farmhouse remained and still looked like the pictures I'd seen of it in Grammy's album. Only the footings to the once enormous barn remained. It must have taken a lot of horses to move the foundation boulders into position. I couldn't quite imagine what a barn that large might have looked like when it was standing. I promised myself to look at the pictures in Grammy's album again when I got home.

At home we had apple trees and pear trees, but no peach trees. Uncle Larry had a slew of peach trees in an orchard across the road from his farm. The orchard, I learned, had once been part of his parents' old homestead but was now his. He had more farmland than I originally thought. I ate so many peaches that I got to visit the outhouse quite often.

We spent some of our time harvesting vegetables, washing them, and storing them in the cool basement. There was a freezer down there. He opened it up and showed me some frozen steaks that had come from one of his slaughtered heifers. When asked what I wanted for supper, I told him that steak would do just fine. What a supper!

During supper, Uncle Larry decided that it was time to make some peach ice cream. He had motorized his ice cream maker and had all the ingredients needed: plenty of ice from the freezer, fresh cream, fresh peaches, sugar, and some salt to add to the ice. After stuffing ice and salt around the sides of the ice-cream maker, we waited for thirty minutes before we took a look. The vanilla ice cream with small chunks of peaches swirled throughout was ready.

The ice-cream maker had done its job. We took what we needed and then covered it over with a heavy towel to keep the rest of the ice cream cold. With our bowls full and a large glass of iced tea, we headed for the front porch. We each had at least three helpings and slept like babies that night.

While driving though the woods behind Uncle Larry's farm, we came upon a small, neat building. He told me he had built it as a hunting cottage. The building had wood shingle siding similar to his farmhouse and was about the size of a large garage. It had a stove, a brick chimney, and a fireplace for warm winter fires when he stayed there overnight during hunting season. I was amazed at what single guys do with their spare time. *When I get older, maybe I'll stay single and live the good life like he does,* I thought.

The only time I was left alone on the farm was when Uncle Larry noticed some people running across the open field at the old farm down the road. We could see in the distance that a tractor was stopped in the field, and it looked as though the people were heading for it. Uncle Larry asked me to stay with Mutt, and he drove his tractor down the road and into the same open field.

I watched for at least a half hour. It looked as if they were working on the double harrow behind the tractor. It was warm, so Mutt and I headed for the basement and the freezer full of goodies. We ended up on the porch eating ice cream together.

A couple of hours later, Uncle Larry drove back into the driveway and parked the tractor in the garage. I offered him some ice cream, but he quietly declined and headed for the sink to wash his hands with the magic Lava soap.

Uncle Larry said nothing about the event until the next morning when he returned from visiting the old farmhouse. I asked what had happened, and he told me that the neighbor's son had been riding on the harrow behind the tractor and had fallen between the harrows. He mentioned that most people loaded their harrows with heavy rocks and chained them down so that the harrow blades could easily cut through the soil. I asked him how badly the boy had been hurt. I saw the troubled expression on his face as he sadly told me that the boy's injuries were very serious. He was still in control but obviously quite upset; I asked no more questions. The day was quiet and sad.

The next morning, after we were awakened by the birds' singing, he named each bird by its music. The mourning doves seemed to chirp the most. I went to the window looking for them, but instead, I spotted deer grazing under a tree next to the house. They had beautiful, dark coats but no antlers. I guess they were just as hungry as I was.

We cleaned up, and headed to the barn to do our chores. I was careful not to do my normal talking and waited for Uncle Larry to speak. I waited a long time. With the work routines already established, we just went about our chores and then cleaned up for breakfast.

At breakfast, Uncle Larry talked a little about the accident—but only a little. He said the two brothers were hard workers, but sometimes they took too many shortcuts. I could see that he felt the accident could have been avoided if they had just taken the time to load the harrows with rocks as most folks did.

After washing the breakfast dishes, we worked in the barn for a while and then headed out to collect more wood for winter. We never talked about the accident again, which was okay with me. I preferred focusing on the current events and not reliving sad ones over and over again.

As the week passed, I fell in love with the smells of the farm. The kitchen smelled like fresh milk. The coolness of the basement combined the smell of different fresh vegetables, making me feel as if I were out in the garden in the cool, early morning. The hay smell in the barn made me want to drop what I was doing and lie down on a stack of hay and take a little nap.

One evening as my week's visit was coming to a close, Uncle Larry asked me if I was interested in staying on for a few more days, or a second week. With great delight and hoping my parents would give their permission, I said, "Sure I am."

He called my mom and she told him she'd get back to him. I was surprised he had asked. And I was even more surprised that Mom hadn't immediately taken him up on his offer.

I didn't ask Uncle Larry why he wasn't doing carpenter work while I was there, but it crossed my mind. Part of the joy of being on the farm was his consistent presence. Because my dad was gone so much in the afternoons and evenings, I'd taken it for granted that he'd eventually have to go do carpenter work for someone. I decided that for once I didn't need to know. I guess Uncle Larry was having an impact on me.

When Mom finally called, we talked. She had a lot of questions for a lady who didn't usually have a lot to say. I was amazed that she actually missed me. But I guess that's what moms do. Even with other children at home, they miss the one who's away.

I stayed an extra three days and then Uncle Larry took me home. He seemed to have enjoyed my company, and that made me feel good. I had absorbed everything about Uncle Larry's farm and his way of life. It wasn't just the country or the farm; it was also his demeanor. I knew I could never be as quiet and collected as he was, but I had enjoyed just being near and with him, and I was thankful for his generosity and graciousness.

—\\\\\\—

My next visit to the farm was in late August. The first thing Uncle Larry did upon my arrival was to show me his new workshop. He had built it in the middle of the field next to the farmhouse. It was larger than his hunting cottage—more like the size of his garage. He was excited as he identified each of the new tools he'd set up in the shop, and then explained what he used each one for.

We worked in the shop for two days running rough hardwood boards through the planer. And then, using the table saw, we stripped the edges of the boards. Uncle Larry said he was going to use much of the hardwood for building cabinets for a customer.

I had never seen him as enthused about anything before. I'm sure he'd been planning it for a long time. He appeared to make good use of his time, not wanting to waste any of it. Time was treated as if it were scarce. He didn't talk about doing things; he just did them every day.

He was so much like his sister, my grandmother—busy, busy, busy. When I first spent time with him, I thought his focus on getting meaningful things done all of the time might have something to do with his heart condition, but later I came to believe it was his style, and I liked it.

During that visit, we also spent a good deal of the time storing hay in the barn. We ate the same type food we had eaten during my first visit, plus we made some apple cider.

Squeezing the juice out of apples is easy when you have the right tools. And we did. The device looked like a rubbish can made of wire screening. The screen encircled an area of about two and a half feet and stood three feet tall. The screened enclosure rested on a cast-iron base with grooves in it to catch the juice and direct it to a waiting jug. Apples were squeezed down into the fenced area by a cast-iron top. The cast-iron top and bottom were held together by a three-foot threaded, metal bolt. At the top of the threaded bolt was a ring that allowed us to place a bat-like handle in it so that we had leverage to turn the metal bolt, thereby squeezing the two bases together. This squeezing process quickly turned the apples into juice. We filled gallon jugs with the juice and used cheesecloth to filter out all of the pulp and seeds as we poured it from one jug into another.

We made gallons of apple juice. I noticed that some of the apples weren't too fresh and some had some bugs in them. Uncle Larry said that they provided the protein and tart flavor and helped to later change the apple juice into a more flavorful beverage—apple cider. I drank it until I was full. Again, I spent more time visiting the outhouse. Why can't I do anything in moderation?

Uncle Larry's cousins, Vern and Alex, were his neighbors. They visited us and we returned their visit. They lived in the smallest house I had ever seen, so small that we didn't even go inside. I wondered how two brothers could live together in such a tiny house. Years later, I found out that Alex had married, and the three of them lived there together.

Just a thought, but maybe Alex and his wife honeymooned in Uncle Larry's hunting cottage. Seriously though, I've learned that many people do with what the family has and do it quietly and privately. That was something I should learn how to do.

—m—

Uncle Larry's brother Richard, unlike Uncle Larry, looked like their dad with long, thick, dark hair. But he was short like Uncle Larry. Grammy took me along a few times when she visited Richard in the nursing home, which was not too far away from Uncle Larry's. We first stopped at the farm and traded fresh items for canned or frozen ones, and then we went on to the nursing home.

Those were unusual visits for me. Up until that time in my life, I had only known one alcoholic—our neighbor Dakin. I didn't know that I had a relative who was an alcoholic. No one ever talked about Richard, and I only visited him with my grandmother. It was like a secret side of the family. No one hushed it up; it just wasn't spoken about when we got together.

The visits to see Richard were not pleasant. The objective was clear. It was to make sure he was properly cared for. Grammy was very upset with the nursing staff whenever she detected the smell of urine on either him or his bedding. It was even worse when she checked him for bedsores and found them. In no uncertain terms, she let them know how displeased she was and demanded better care for him.

Unfortunately, she found it necessary to move him twice to newer and cleaner nursing homes. Even though she worked full-time, she took on the responsibility of overseeing the care of her ill brother. Her love and care for others overwhelmed me, and the memory of how she lived to serve others still does.

—◊—

Uncle Larry eventually married when he was in his late fifties. When I heard that he had gotten married, I was immediately happy for them and didn't think about his heart condition. I assumed he'd found a successful medical solution for it and moved on. However, just as the military doctors had predicted, he lived less than two years and died of a heart attack. Reflecting back on Uncle Larry makes me feel good about him and his choices. With courage, he faced life every day taking on one problem at a time. I still want to be more like him.

Farm ready

CHAPTER 22

Meaningful Projects

Some people referred to our street as Cemetery Road even though its legal name was Franklin Street. The cemetery, with its tall entrance pillars made of cement and smooth round rocks, occupied both sides of the street and dominated the whole lower end of the street.

I walked by that cemetery many times during daylight, but in the early evening as darkness set in, the shadows from the large gravestones played games with my mind. One time, as my penalty for having lost at checkers, Grandpa made me learn the Twenty-third Psalm. I repeated it over and over again as I briskly walked past the stone entrances. Knowing that home was only a half mile away, just over the railroad tracks and up the hill, I sped up and never looked back. Two huge maple trees in our front yard identified our house, so you couldn't miss it; but at night those trees made the front very dark and shadowy. Even so, I was glad when my feet hit the driveway.

There were three major buildings on our approximately two acres of land: our house, a small garage, and a shed, which some referred to as a small barn. Our garage, with its bowed wooden drive-up ramp, was set back about seventy-five feet from the house and matched the house with its exterior light gray wood shingles and white painted trim.

For a period of time, we had pigs. We kept them behind the garage with the back side of the building serving as part of their pen. They loved to scratch their bodies by rubbing themselves against the garage siding, and they ended up destroying the lower four feet of it. Dad eventually replaced and painted the damaged shingles. I wasn't old enough to help, but I watched him work.

I recall a dream I had during that time. In the dream, I rode the pigs—it wasn't easy. Our pigs often got out of their pen and sauntered over to our neighbor's house and tore up their lawn and garden. This, of course, was not appreciated. Dad finally had enough and they were butchered and the pen torn down. We planted rhubarb and a maple tree in that area. The ground was so fertile that no additional fertilizing was ever needed.

The garage was just a garage—nothing fancy. There was a side door, which could be seen from the back porch of the house, and the two large windows on opposite sides of the garage let enough light in so that you could see to walk around, but you needed overhead lighting to do anything more. A workbench containing Dad's tools was set against the wall, and the farm and yard tools were hung up on the walls. Stored beneath one of the windows was an old chest.

The handmade chest belonged to Pepére. It was about four feet long, three feet tall, and two feet deep. It was stained dark mahogany with shiny brass tacks edging the corners and cover. When opened, the hinged cover was held open by a metal chain.

My ancestors were coppersmiths; the chest was full of tools once used by them in their trade of making copper pots and pans. Most of the tools were wrapped in soft cloths. There were padded hammers, molds of all shapes, and unique cutting tools. I easily imagined my great-great-grandparents traveling with this chest in the back of their wagon as they went from town to town creating and selling their pots and pans to the New Englanders.

Nature and human nature require that children have some area indoors to play, not only during bad weather, but as a place to dream and be creative. No one used this garage except for storing chicken feed and tools. We had no car, therefore, it was basically underutilized.

One rainy day as I played out there on the floor with my army men and other toys, I realized how comfortable and secure it felt; and it could become a special place for me. Every now and then I heard a car go by, but otherwise, it was quiet. I also noticed that Mom and Julie very seldom visited the garage. Whenever I was out there playing, they just stepped out on the porch and hollered, "Jacob, you okay?" I was more than okay!

I learned to leave the side garage door open all the time to make sure they heard my response to their calls. I found that leaving it open discouraged Julie's visits, but the minute I closed it, I had all kinds of company—not just Julie. A closed door seemed to raise everyone's attention and curiosity.

The third building was the old shed. It was located about sixty feet to the left of the garage and further back on the lot. Aside from being dark and full of cobwebs and car parts, it did serve as a storage space for the tractor and provided one of the walls of the pigpen. To me, it looked like an old ranch building. I listened as Dad and Mom talked about how it needed repair, and now that the pigs were gone, maybe it was time to tear it down.

My dad worked very hard physically at the mill. In my opinion, he didn't need any more physically demanding work to do. *Therefore*, I thought, *it was my turn to take on more of the work around home.* So, at supper one evening, I asked my folks if I could tear down the shed.

I had dreamed about it for weeks. Before I asked, I thought through how I'd do it and how I'd respond to their concerns about me being too young. I was overprepared and believed I could convince them that a strong ten-year-old boy like me could do the job.

It was important not to overplay my confidence. I didn't want to end up like General MacArthur. Earlier that year, on April 11th, he had pushed too hard for permission to bomb Chinese cities. He said, "No substitute for victory!" President Truman relieved him of command.

I knew in my heart they appreciated my help in the garden weeding and taking care of the chickens. This was also the first year I was big enough to run the gas-powered cultivator; therefore, I was convinced they wouldn't turn me down because of my lack of strength.

At first, they laughed at my request; then I saw them look at each other. I saw it pass between them, that kind of dawning light that made them stop and focus for just a second. I hoped they were thinking that it wasn't a bad idea.

Dad mentioned how dangerous the job could be with rusty nails all around and the potential of falling off the roof. He went on to say he didn't think kids should spend a lot of their time working because they'd eventually spend the rest of their lives working, and that was enough.

I listened and then described how I planned to take it apart piece by piece. I'd remove every nail before it could hurt anyone. My mom sat quietly and listened. I was dying inside. What if they said no? I hated the word *no* and still do! The only word I hate more than no is the word *can't*.

Dad said, "Let us sleep on it." *I'm halfway there*, I thought, and told myself to just shut up and let Dad and Mom talk it out.

The next day before Dad left for work, he walked me around the shed and said, "No nails on the ground, ever." He gave me a carpenter's apron and helped me put it on. He double folded it because it was much too long and then tied it behind my back. He handed me his hammer and told me to be careful. He was really concerned.

I was in heaven—my first big project. God loves me, He really does! For the rest of the day, I worked on the nails sticking out of the building and just banged around. I was still trying to think through the details of how I'd take it apart piece by piece.

It was going to be a hot summer day and Dad was still asleep. I knew I shouldn't work on the shed until he was rested and awake. So I cooled it until he was up and eating breakfast. By then, it was midmorning and getting warmer by the minute. I started slowly. I was amazed at how hard it was to pull out hundreds of nails and spikes one by one. Dad stopped by and checked my work and showed me where and how to stack the lumber. He was friendly, but I could see he was still concerned.

This was special work for me. It wasn't like weeding the garden or taking care of chickens. This was adult stuff, the kind of work men got paid for, and I was feeling more like a grown-up than a kid and loved it.

The main shed had an attached building in the rear with its own roof. Each roof had to be cleared of shingles and all of the shingle nails pulled. Only then could I begin tearing the roof apart. I found some old, empty paint cans to put the nails into. I was very careful not to fall off the roof or step ladder.

After my Dad left for work, Pepére often stopped by with his thermos bottle in hand. I thought he really liked coffee, that is, until I tasted it once.

It was bitter. I learned later that it had booze in it. No wonder his French nose was red much of the time.

Pepére had retired from working as a weaver in the same woolen mill where my dad worked. He was short in stature, a little over five feet tall, but strong, healthy, and smart. He was almost bald and wore neat straw hats like those you see in pictures of New Orleans musicians. He never remarried after my grandmother's death. A couple of his close friends called him the French Jew because he was so tight with his money.

Pepére was very sociable, had a great laugh, and tried to add value. He'd sit nearby and suggest how to take the building apart, but he never made me think it had to be done his way. He wasn't pushy. Pepére never stayed long; he didn't want to be an imposition.

My dad and Pepére were close friends. They not only fished together but also loved to hunt for deer and turkey in the fall. It was great to sit and listen to their conversations. They were both union men and skeptical of businessmen, in general, and mill owners, in particular. I liked listening to them talk as long as they spoke English, but I was lost when they spoke French.

Pepére spent much of his time either fishing or at the racetrack. He said he never bet to win because he didn't like the odds. He only bet "to show" and usually came home with more money in his pocket than he'd started out with.

Over the years, Pepére owned two boats. He kept them at our place during the winter months and in the spring prepared them for fishing. After he removed the paint and old caulking on his large wooden boat, he re-caulked it with twine and caulking compound. I helped him scrape the paint off, but only he used the blowtorch to remove the hard stuck paint. When he put his boat in the water, the wood swelled and the caulking sealed the joints between the boards. We did some fishing together in both fresh and saltwater, and I loved it when he let me drive the boat. Because of the time spent with him, I later came up with the idea to build a boat for my dad.

One day, he took me to lunch at a Greek restaurant downtown. During lunch, the owner stopped by and they talked about fishing. Pepére told him he hadn't been feeling too well and didn't think that he was going to live much longer. This worried me. When I got home, I waited up for my dad to get home from work, and we talked. I told him what Pepére had said about not feeling well and not living much longer. I also repeated that he said he was having stomach problems.

My dad bent over laughing and said, "No wonder he has stomach problems; he drinks a quart of booze a day!"

This was news to me, and based on my small sample of the taste of booze in his thermos, I couldn't understand why anyone would drink that stuff. I never saw him drunk or even tipsy. I guess he was just a "social" drinker as I had heard others describe themselves. In later years, he slowed down on his drinking. I believe it had a lot to do with his stomach pain and maybe even more to do with the cost of the liquor.

The summer days passed too quickly; the old wood was stacked as Dad had specified. I had filled lots of old paint cans with the rusty nails and spikes. Some were so rusted that they wouldn't come out. I learned to pound them into the wood, but I still worried about whether or not Dad would approve. One day, he came out and examined some of the wood with the spikes and nails driven deep into them and said nothing. I was relieved!

I placed all of the torn-up shingles in metal rubbish buckets and hauled them in the wheelbarrow out to the street, hoping the city trash collectors would pick them up. They did and without a complaint.

After the project was finished and before summer ended, a fellow came by and asked to take the stacked wood off my dad's hands for free. He wanted some of the boards for a project he was working on, and he was going to cut up the rest for firewood. I certainly hoped he'd check closely for nails before he did any cutting. We were all pleased when the wood was gone; the yard looked so much better without the ugly, old shed.

I was learning that I liked space and hated clutter. I also discovered a little about how many unknowns you can run into in tackling new projects. More important, I learned that meaningful projects can be exciting adventures. A subtle thing I learned about myself was that people who love you really want to help you, but I found it hard letting them help me. I knew this was pride but didn't know how to overcome it.

—∿—

We had cats to keep the mice from eating too much of the feed, but obviously they didn't get all of them. Many people called them field mice. I never knew the difference between house and field mice. I knew it didn't make any difference to my sister—she just screamed every time she saw one.

One day my dad stated, "You're feeling pretty grown up now with your project completed, aren't you?"

He seemed serious, and since I didn't feel he was making fun of me, I said, "Sometimes."

"Okay then. I've got another project for you, but you will have to be very careful. Can I trust you?"

"Sure you can, Dad." I was complimented. What could this project be?

Dad described the problem. We had too many cats to feed now that another litter had been born. Dad went on to say that our neighbor flushed new kittens down the toilet, but he couldn't handle that. He said we needed to find another way of getting rid of them. We had all talked about giving them away and came to the conclusion that we'd done that many times before and everyone we knew now had cats. At that time, there wasn't any animal shelter to take them to. I understood that we couldn't afford to feed a lot of cats.

Dad, having made his decision, said, "I want you to dig a two-foot-deep hole down near the stone wall and place the kittens on the bottom. The mother will follow and stay in the hole with the kittens. Shooting them will kill them instantly and they won't suffer. We need to kill the mother, as well as the kittens, because she never stops breeding."

He handed me a bird shotgun shell and said that it had forty to fifty small, steel pellets in it. He wanted me to wait until the mother and the kittens were comfortable, and then I was to kill all of them with one shot. I was not to waste a second shell because they were expensive.

I gulped when he told me to do it today. He asked if I anticipated any problems and repeated his concern about safety. Then Dad grabbed his lunch bucket off the porch step and headed down the driveway to catch his ride to work.

He trusts me with his shotgun, so I can't let him down, I thought. I was surprised by the project. What does he have on his mind? This must be some kind of a test. I went up into the attic and got the shotgun and stood there for a moment. What if I miss? I grabbed three extra shells, stuck them in my pocket, and headed back to my sanctuary.

As I continued thinking about it, I realized it wasn't like Dad to test me; I came to the conclusion that he just didn't have time to do it, and I tried to adjust my head set. I grabbed a shovel and headed to the back lot. I dug the hole as instructed but wondered if the cat would stay in the hole with her kittens. Then I went back into the house and to the kitchen where the kittens were in a cardboard box beside the stove. I picked up the box and the mother followed me out and across the open field to the hole. I quickly ran back to the garage, grabbed the shotgun, and hurried back to the hole. I was getting more nervous by the minute.

The mother was dancing around the box and my legs and appeared to know something was up—or maybe it was just my nerves. I placed the small box of kittens in the bottom of the hole and waited. We had cut the top of the box off so the mother could walk in and out, but the sides were too tall for the little ones to leave.

The mother eventually entered the hole and then jumped out again. She did this several times. If this was a test planned by my dad, it was to test my patience. I waited and waited and tried desperately to think of some other way to get rid of them, but I couldn't come to closure on any way that would be less painful. After deciding the mother was never going to settle down, I tried to angle the weapon to shoot her as she walked back into the box. I again waited, and waited, and then finally said to myself, *that's it*, and fired.

The mother was paralyzed in her hindquarter but was able to pull herself to the edge of the hole and look up at me for help. This was supposed to have been pain free for her and her kittens. I had messed up and she paid the price. I quickly shot again and then checked each kitten and the mother. They were all at peace. I threw the empty shell casings into the hole and filled it in.

On the way back to the garage, I wondered if my dad had counted the number of shells in the box upstairs before he left for work. Pepére would have. Thank God Dad never asked how it went. I'm sure it would have been hard to tell the truth.

With the shed now gone, I looked forward to making the garage much more functional. Having turned eleven years old during that summer, I thought that my next project should be making a rack that would hang from the rafters to store the good lumber that had been stacked against the back wall and floor of the garage for a long time. I'd seen this done in Grandpa's garage. I talked to my dad about the project. He said it wasn't necessary, but if I felt I needed to do it, "Go to it."

It took me a few days to select the stringers that would be strong enough to hold all of the weight, and then I selected the right bolts to hold them together. As construction progressed, I got very tired working from ladders and found that stacking the lumber on the finished rack was also very clumsy work. I felt off balance most of the time. So I slowed down and took my time, for this was wearing me out.

What a difference the storage rack made in the garage. The cluttered look was gone and there was lots of space. I kept the place swept and the windows clean. I felt good about what I had accomplished, but there was something missing. There was no ambiance. My next project was to include getting music out there. What is a clubhouse or workshop without good music?

There were three large items stacked against the left side of the garage. The first item was a living room stove that had been there since Pepére sold his home. It was like an oversized space heater. The outer shell was black and deep red. Inside the shell was an actual wood-burning stove. We kept it covered with a blanket so that it wouldn't get scratched. It was beautiful! Pepére now lived in an apartment downtown and had no need for it. There was never any talk about selling it. I figured he kept it for sentimental reasons. With this in mind, I guessed there was nothing I could do to get rid of it. I asked a few questions and danced around the subject with my folks and Pepére but got no bites, so I let it alone.

Next to the stove was a very tall container of chicken feed. It was almost as big as the stove and had a reasonably tight cover. Occasionally, when I dipped the trowel into the container for grain, a mouse would pop out of the feed. I figured when I opened the cover he'd bury himself. When he came to the surface, I tried to kill him with the trowel, but he usually made it out of the feed bin and raced around the garage. I never did catch or kill one. The garage, being built on blocks, was elevated about eighteen inches above the ground. I'm sure he had a nest under there somewhere.

The third item along the wall in the garage was a very large radio that stood about four feet tall. It was similar to the kind of radio you saw on television when they showed and played President Roosevelt's announcement that the Japanese had bombed Pearl Harbor. The antique radio belonged to Pepére and I asked him if I could have it. He gave it to me but said it didn't work. I really wanted some music in my private world, so I removed some of the plug-in tubes from the back of the ancient radio and walked down to Western Auto and had them tested. I was in luck; only one was bad, and I had enough money from mowing lawns to purchase the replacement tube. I plugged all the tubes back in and was delightfully amazed when the radio actually worked—but I could barely hear it.

Dad suggested an antenna; so I unrolled some wire that he had hanging on the back wall, connected it to the back of the radio, and tacked the other end to one of the garage rafters. The volume and reception were perfect and transformed the garage into a warm and friendly place to work and have fun.

When Pepére visited and heard the radio playing, he just smiled. I had no idea what he was thinking. Was it his memories of the radio playing earlier in his life, or was it the pleasure of sharing his radio with me? I'll never know, but the music was wonderful.

The radio took up too much space, so I decided to take it apart and rebuild it. I wanted a smaller cabinet but one big enough to accommodate the speakers and all the components. There were some pieces of plywood in the basement that I could use. The cabinet would be two feet wide, eighteen inches high, and twelve inches deep. I hoped it would eventually look like a tabletop radio, and it certainly wouldn't take up nearly as much garage space.

I spent two weeks measuring, cutting, sanding, staining, and varnishing. It was not an easy project but it looked cool, was functional, and I set it on top of Pepére's beautiful living room stove. When the radio played loud music, the speakers vibrated. It was interesting.

The garage was ready for a car, if my parents decided to buy one, or it was ready for my next project. Either way, I had a beautiful place to play, work, and hide out—plus it had ambiance.

CHAPTER 23

Economics

The four seasons of the year are significantly different in New Hampshire: Winters are characteristically cold and windy with lots of snow and ice. Spring is usually cool and rainy but has some warm days, resulting in budding trees and blooming crocuses and daffodils. Summers can be quite comfortable or unbearably hot and muggy but either way, usually too short. Fall is the best season of all. The air turns crisp and refreshingly cool, except for an Indian summer day tucked in there. And before dropping their leaves, the trees display their palette of glorious fall colors.

Many of our parents lived through the Depression and their experiences had an amazing impact on us children. Lights were to be turned off when you left a room, and often one light in a room was considered enough. Doors were to be closed to keep the cold out, and windows were to be opened to let the cool breeze in. Many still preferred to walk or bike rather than drive. Horses were preferred to tractors. *Homegrown* meant grown in one's garden, as well as grown in the good ole USA.

My aunt had a saying regarding saving water and the toilet: When it is yellow, let it mellow; when it is brown, flush it down. You didn't take things for granted. Relatives and friends were considered a critical survival resource and were to be cherished and protected.

Jobs were scarce. It was critical to have a craft or skill in order to maximize your hourly income. At our local woolen mill, weavers earned more than fixers, fixers more than spinners, and so forth. Second-and third-shift workers were paid shift incentives.

My dad worked there as a loom fixer. Basically, he was a machinist and repairman. The loom parts were very heavy and he often came home with a back problem. Work was not steady. Some months Dad only worked one or two weeks; therefore, no one in our family took incoming cash for granted. He worked second shift for the hourly premium. Even though working that shift separated him from the family during the evenings, that was a sacrifice we all had to make to survive.

To stay liquid, my parents paid off their mortgage as soon as they could and kept our utility bills as small as possible. The key to survival was to have as little fixed overhead as possible. It was never how much you earned, but how much you could keep in the family that counted. Before we ever hired a vendor to do something for us, we first thought about whether or not there was a family member who could teach us how to do it or do it for us.

There was a fully insulated cold-storage room in the north corner of the basement. It contained a large freezer and wood shelves for storing the fresh fruits and vegetables that we had harvested. We also froze meat. These items were all needed for our survival during the winter. The homegrown fruits and vegetables were the foundation of each meal. Mom used them to make soups and salads to take the bite off our hunger before serving the main course.

We had an acre or more of potatoes, beets, snap beans, pea beans, corn, popcorn, carrots, tomatoes, strawberries, blackberries, rhubarb, onions, peppers, pear trees, apple trees, and many items I have forgotten.

We canned lots of our fruits and vegetables. I recall that canning day was a time when the family got together. As children and grandchildren, we worked with the adults using our limited skills to help them complete the necessary tasks. When they canned tomatoes, the kitchen was full of sterile jars on the table, seals and covers on the kitchen counters, and large pots on the stove. The sink was full of tomatoes being cleaned and prepared for cooking. When cooked, the jars were filled and sealed and stored in the basement on the hanging shelves beside the staircase. Jars of homemade jams and jellies were also kept there. This process was repeated with each canning event.

When I wanted something extra to eat, which was most of the time, I pulled up carrots from the garden and washed them under the outside faucet. I also enjoyed raw potatoes from the cold storage, once the eyes were broken off. Sometimes I grabbed a can of frozen orange juice from the freezer and ate it like ice cream. I didn't grow up hungry, but I do admit to a limited and healthy diet.

My favorite vegetable was popcorn, which was easy to harvest. You picked it, shucked it, and hung the cobs to dry. When it was dry, you removed the kernels by wringing the corn cob with your hands, allowing the kernels to drop into a container. Then we filled freezer bags with the kernels. We popped the kernels in a long-handled, metal basket over the stove. You couldn't beat the taste of that hot, buttered popcorn. It was fantastic!

We had pigs, mature egg-laying chickens, and pullet chickens for eating. I remember inserting little pellets into the back of the necks of the pullet chickens to fatten them up. I moved their cages around so that their fertilizer wouldn't be concentrated too much and burn the soil.

The potatoes in the cold storage were not just for eating. We used some of them for planting in the spring. To insure that they'd have sufficient bulk to make it through the winter, their eyes, which became roots when you planted them, had to be removed. The planting was done by cutting each potato into quarters and planting the pieces about eighteen inches apart.

Cash was scarce; therefore, we harvested and preserved what we could to survive. Although many might have described us as poor, we never went hungry. When we ate meals together, we celebrated the blessing of having all of the fruits, vegetables, eggs, and meat that we needed. All of this was the key to our survival. It was important that Dad worked outside the home; however, it was not as reliable as it needed to be for survival.

The fall hunting season was an opportunity to have fun and add some protein to the freezer. We killed deer for food and traded their hides for buckskin gloves or hats. Learning to hunt was a special adventure, and shooting my first deer was a heart-thumping experience.

My dad owned a 38/55 lever-action rifle. It had a hexagon barrel and was very heavy, but that's what I hunted with for three years. He hunted with a new lever Marlin 35 carbine rifle. It was a beautiful weapon.

On the first day of hunting season, when I was fourteen years old, my dad invited me to go with him to hunt near a game reserve. He had purchased a J. C. Higgins 12-gage shotgun a couple of years before in order to hunt wild turkeys. He gave me that shotgun to use, which was half the weight of the old 38/55 rifle.

Dad was a very careful hunter. I respected his experience in the infantry during the war, so I listened carefully to his instructions. We walked into the woods and followed a logging road up a small hill. He sat me on a tree stump and said he'd walk a circle, pointing as he talked, and then come back to me. I was to sit still and if there were any deer around they'd most likely head in my direction.

I sat quietly on the stump watching the sun come up. It was a beautiful, cold, clear and quiet morning. The stump was on the highest area of ground around for about two hundred yards, so I had a nice view. A stone wall ran parallel to the logging road, and just beyond the stone wall was an open field. There, standing in the field, facing the wall and looking up at me, was a deer.

I couldn't tell if it was a buck or a doe, but I knew it didn't make any difference—meat was protein. I hadn't experienced buck fever before. It started in my stomach and moved north to my upper body. In just a few seconds, I felt nervous and sweaty. I aimed about eight inches above the deer's neck and slowly turned the safety off. My heart was thumping like nothing I'd experienced before. I squeezed and the deer jumped up in the air, sprang over the wall, and headed for the logging road.

After flipping the bolt to reload the weapon, I ran down the loggers' road to meet the deer. The buck was running through the small trees about fifty feet from the road. He was thrashing his head and standing tall on his hind legs. I aimed at his neck and fired again. This time he slumped to the ground. I walked over slowly and touched his head with the barrel of my rifle. He didn't move.

Dad arrived, winded but with still enough air in his lungs to say, "Stay away!" He jumped between me and the deer and pushed me back away from it. He checked. The deer was dead—I had killed an eight-point buck.

Dad looked at me and said, "Didn't I tell you not to leave the stump?" I wanted to say something but laughed instead; after catching his breath, he also laughed.

We tied a rope to the antlers and swung the rope over a tree branch near the logging road. It took both of us to hoist the deer high enough into the air to begin cleaning it.

The internal organs of the deer amazed me. They were not only perfectly formed and clean but were compactly organized and protected in a sack. I wondered how anyone could doubt God's existence. The deer was still very warm inside. I then understood how men's lives were saved in the frontier by covering themselves with the skins of newly killed deer, bear, or buffalo.

Dad drove the car up the logging road. We laid the buck over the car fender and tied it down. I tied a tag to his ear just in case we were stopped by the ranger on the way home.

The deer was too big to hang in the garage, so we laid a twenty-four-foot ladder against the garage and hung the deer from it. After taking pictures, we let it set for a while and went in and ate breakfast. I was glowing and couldn't stop looking out the window at the deer.

Later, we skinned it, cut it up, and wrapped each piece individually before placing them in the freezer. We shared the deer meat with relatives, friends, and neighbors when they came over to visit. Deer meat has a much stronger flavor than beef. My mom cooked it with lots of onions and seasoning and sometimes mixed it with other meats to make it more tasteful. When she was done, you usually didn't know you were eating venison.

—◊◊◊—

If and when you wanted to make a large purchase, like a car, you saved up for it, paid for it with cash, and did most of the repair work yourself. We didn't have a car of our own until my last two years of high school. When my folks finally decided to make the purchase, Dad showed me the three one-hundred-dollar bills he was using to purchase the four-door Plymouth sedan. I was impressed!

Grocery shopping was done once a week and only for those things we couldn't provide for ourselves. Shopping for clothes was limited because my mom and grandmother sewed and were able to make dresses; coats; men's shirts; heavy, lined wool shirts; and most of the children's clothing. Of course, items like shoes, nonwool socks, underwear, and purses had to be purchased.

We had a small vegetable stand in front of our house, and most of the cash from summer and fall sales was used for back-to-school clothes. My sneakers never lasted long. I looked forward to selling potatoes and fruits so that I could buy a new pair every year. This environment was focused on the basics of survival, but it didn't limit my dreams.

Even as a youth, I enjoyed physical labor and searched for jobs that created cash. When I got up early to mow lawns or shovel snow, I recall my dad often asking, "Why do you do this? It embarrasses me. Why don't you just go and have fun with your friends and not work so hard? Once you grow up, you'll have to work hard for the rest of your life."

I told him I loved the feeling of having cash in my wallet and loose change in my pocket because cash to me was freedom. I'd had my fill of playing as a kid, and I liked working because it made me feel good about myself.

Everyone living in New Hampshire knows about the four different seasons because they experience them. Their experiences, however, do not always reflect a full appreciation of what the seasons really do to the land. Every spring and fall we plowed with our old, single-plow tractor. And every year the plow turned over new rocks, which we put into a wheelbarrow and wheeled to the stone wall at the back of the lot. The freezing and thawing of the soil created a natural movement of rocks so that each spring and summer I could predict having a new group of rocks to haul down to the stone wall.

If you have traveled much of New Hampshire, you've seen many beautiful stone walls. If you look into the fields surrounding the walls, you'll still see more rocks waiting to be placed on those walls. It's a never-ending cycle, not a onetime lot-cleaning exercise, which one would expect. I have a lot of respect for farmers, in general, but more specifically for those hardworking New England farmers.

Jacob, Monty, and eight-point buck

CHAPTER 24

Harvesting

No matter the season or reason, harvesting time was a special event. In most parts of eastern New Hampshire, wild blueberries grew along the roads and near the woods and were available to anyone for the picking. They grew in the right-of-ways, so almost no one complained when people stopped and picked a few buckets. The larger blueberries seemed to grow in the mountains, which was only fair because of the cleaner air and more sun. The plans for the day might be to take a drive, enjoy the scenery, stop at relatives for a visit, and pick some berries on the way home. Good eating and good health.

For a few years in the late fall, Dad cut a groove and tapped the maple trees in our front yard for maple syrup. Mom boiled the sap until it reached the right sugar concentration and temperature, and then she filtered the syrup through a special cloth. It didn't take long before it was ready to be bottled and used.

We gathered eggs every day. Chicken feed and weekly shells kept the chickens healthy; thus protein was available at the end of a short walk down the path. We killed the chickens periodically. Our family, however, had two uniquely different methods for doing this.

Dad worked part-time at the turkey farm two houses up. There he learned to kill the turkeys by inserting a sharp knife through the mouth into the hanging turkey's brain. It was instant death and Dad was always most comfortable with the least painful methodology. He required that

I used that method on our chickens. After they were dead, we pulled the feathers out and then singed the hair off by lighting a small cup of alcohol. The feathers that fell to the floor were very clean, as long as the chicken house was clean, and it was my job to see that it was.

One day under Grammy's clothesline, Grandpa taught me another way to kill chickens. He had me lay the chicken's head and neck across a chopping block and cut the head off using a small ax. I was to immediately dip the chicken in a bucket of steaming hot water and then hang it by its feet on the clothesline.

Even headless, the chickens sometimes had other ideas. It wasn't a bit fun chasing a headless chicken around the backyard. Grandpa laughed and told me to hurry up or it would be tough to pull the feathers out. This happened twice, but I eventually dunked them in the hot bucket. He was right; pulling the feathers out was tougher.

Since the feathers came off so easily when I did it right, I suggested the process to my dad. However, cleaning up the feathers was easier with Dad's process. Either way, having chicken available whenever you needed it was wonderfully convenient and inexpensive.

The harvesting time for lettuce, tomatoes, peppers, onions, and carrots ran from June through August and could be done at your leisure. If you had your own garden, it meant you didn't have to shop every few days for fresh vegetables, they were less expensive, and they tasted so much better. I'm sure that is why many people today have their own victory gardens.

To me, the most important thing about harvesting was that it was done outdoors. When I was outside, there was always the possibility of something happening. Our raspberry bushes were as tall as I was and prickly, though not as prickly as the blackberry bushes. One day, as I picked raspberries near our apple trees, I heard a thumping sound. I turned around and saw two huge workhorses running across the open field not fifty yards from me. I stood there frozen.

Those workhorses came from the Carters' farm about a quarter mile away. They hardly ever got loose and I was surprised and spooked by their arrival. I didn't see anyone chasing them. Twenty minutes later the Carters showed up on our back steps and asked Mom if she had seen them. The horses didn't stay long, and although they caused a commotion, they appeared to take pleasure in their freedom. One was black as midnight and the other white as new snow. Once I got over the fear of being trampled to death, I enjoyed watching them run free.

My favorite harvesting job was digging potatoes. Because I had weeded them with my mom and sister during the growing season, I had a vested interest in them. As I hoed, I imagined that I was digging for gold. I used a potato fork and pulled it through the elevated bed. This leveled the loam and in the process pulled out the remaining weeds.

Usually, the potato plants were dead, but sometimes I had to separate the potatoes from the plants. The shapes of the potatoes were numerous: double knuckled, ninety-degree knuckled, half-dollar sized, or perfectly round. It made no difference, we used them for food and as seeds for next spring's planting.

Corn and popcorn were bulky to harvest and filled a bushel basket quickly. Raccoons love corn, so sometimes there was damaged corn, especially closer to the woods. I found that spending time in the corn field frequently led to disturbing large snakes as they searched for field mice.

—∞—

The hottest and hardest work was harvesting hay. It didn't take long to get Uncle Larry's hay cut and stored because he didn't have a large herd of cows to feed. It was a bigger project at a farm I spent a week at during my early teens. The farm, which was in the nearby town of Farmington, belonged to my mother's high school girlfriend.

I'd never met a child of the state before. Troy was very strong and worked hard as he lifted hay on his hayfork to the top of the truck where I pulled it up and spread it. His temporary guardian drove the truck and helped with the harvesting.

One day, after we finished loading the truck and were headed back to the barn, Troy and I spent some time talking about his life moving from home to home. He said he didn't mind being a ward of the state but was anxious to find a permanent place to live. It was getting late and since it was our last load for the day, his guardian decided to have supper before putting the hay in the barn. We stayed on top of the load of hay for a little while and continued our conversation.

He said something about me being slow, and we started to wrestle as guys do. Before we knew it, we fell off the hay truck and crashed to the ground. I was fine, but he landed on his head and just laid there—out cold. I ran to get help. As I ran, I prayed that he would be okay. By the time we all got back to the truck, Troy was sitting up and moving around.

They examined him closely and made him follow their finger with his eyes until they were convinced he was all right. I got a lecture about being a high-risk guest. I was told I could have eliminated their income from the state if he'd been hurt. Then I realized why he was looking for a permanent place to live and, hopefully, with a family that had their priorities right.

The next afternoon we happened to be in the house all alone, and Troy suggested we go up into the attic and have some root beer. It was in large bottles. We opened a bottle and drank some of it—warm. Troy said that they had made it with sugar, baker's yeast, and some extract. He further explained that the root beer was stored in the attic during its carbonation process. We quit drinking it and went out to the barn. It didn't take long before I had a stomachache. My stomach gurgled and was upset all evening long. I had so much gas in my system that I thought I'd die.

I said, "Thanks a lot, Troy," and concluded that drinking root beer before it was ready was a dumb thing to do, and that I got what I deserved. I often thought about Troy during the following winter and hoped he had found a caring, permanent home.

Jacob cultivating

CHAPTER 25

Almost Teamwork

Our single-plow tractor was a mutt made up of parts from other vehicles. Its basic body and engine was a 1926 Chevrolet. The four-cylinder engine powered the rear bus wheels through two transmissions. The two transmissions really slowed the tractor down, but the huge bus wheels and tires gave it traction. With snow chains on the tires, the tractor could pull almost anything. It had no muffler, so it was very loud.

The plow was lifted up and down by a winch and cable that was powered by the tractor engine. The cable traveled from the winch to the back of the tractor through a four-foot tower with a pulley in it. The only floor on the tractor was under and in front of the driver's seat. This was a poor man's tractor; nevertheless, twice a year it did what we needed it to do and very inexpensively.

One year, my grandmother asked Dad to plow her garden. My grandfather usually plowed their garden with horses, but he'd fallen off my uncle's roof while helping him build his house and wasn't fit enough to handle horses.

Dad decided to plow their garden on Saturday, but the winch that lifted the plow didn't work. So he asked me to help him by lifting the plow at the end of each furrow. I was complimented that he wanted me to help. We'd finally be a team on a project. I was delighted!

As a temporary solution until he could get the winch repaired, he had rigged up a hanging chain and hook to keep the plow suspended in the air. The plow was hitched to a steel bar that ran across the back of the tractor. I was to stand and ride on that bar while holding on to the tower in the center of it.

Dad drove the slow tractor down to my grandmother's and I unhooked the plow from the chain. He plowed the first furrow. At the end of the furrow, he backed up a little to loosen the plow. I stepped down off the bar and lifted the plow about three feet in the air and hooked it to the hanging chain. And then I climbed back up on the bar and stood behind him so that he could see to back down the furrow.

We had developed a good routine and then the rain started. It wasn't heavy rain, but it was steady. The tractor wheels started slipping, so we attached snow chains to the bus tires and continued the process. We were about half done. When we came to the end of the furrow, I lifted the wet plow and hooked it up and jumped on the back bar of the tractor. Unfortunately, I slipped and fell into the furrow. Before I could get up, the tractor was slowly being backed over me. I could see up through the tractor frame. Since Dad hadn't seen me fall, he assumed that I was safely behind him and, therefore, was focused on shifting and backing up. I screamed, but with no muffler on the tractor he couldn't hear me.

My feet were buried in the muddy furrow under the left, rear wheel of the tractor. The snow chain on the tractor wheel was headed toward my knees, and I screamed again. I couldn't hear myself scream and wondered if I was in a dream. I hated those tires and twisted and turned under the tractor trying to avoid getting directly run over. I couldn't feel a thing as the rear wheel was slowly burying my upper legs and a portion of my body in the mud. I kept screaming up into the frame of the tractor and finally our eyes met. Thank God there was almost no floor on the tractor. Suddenly, I felt hopeful.

Dad's eyes were wide open with shock and disbelief. He stopped the tractor. He shifted again, but it was still in reverse and it backed up. He immediately stopped it. He looked down at me with those "I'm sorry, I'm really sorry" eyes. I said nothing and waited. He finally shifted into forward and drove off me.

He carefully lifted me out of the mud and carried me to my grandmother's car. I was a wet and muddy mess. He ran in for the keys and then drove us to the nearest doctor's office on Main Street, just a few miles away.

The doctor and nurse gently and cautiously cleaned me up. I couldn't feel my legs. After checking me over, the doctor assured us that there were no broken bones, but my muscles and tendons were badly bruised. I'd need to exercise them to get them back into shape. He believed I'd fully recover, but as I got older, I'd probably experience some pain in my legs. I felt blessed because the mud appeared to have absorbed much of the tractor's weight.

Dad eventually carried me back to the car and told me that he was going back in to see the doctor. I was suspicious about their meeting without me, but Dad saw it in my eyes and told me not to worry for it wasn't about me. He had never lied to me before, and I certainly hoped he wasn't really going back in to talk about any permanent damage to my legs.

I experienced a prickling sensation as the sense of feeling returned to my legs. It was as if they were waking up from having been asleep. It was uncomfortable and somewhat painful, but it was certainly something I could handle.

At first, exercising and walking were quite painful, but as time passed and the muscles and tendons healed, the pain went away and I got my legs back in shape. As it took time for my legs to heal, it also took some time for both of us to stop having bad dreams about the accident. Only once after healing did Dad talk to me about the accident, and I don't recall him ever driving the tractor again.

There were two things about the accident that caused me regret: First, I caused my dad unnecessary pain. And second, we failed to finish a joint project. I felt we needed to find ways to stay close, and we had missed a golden opportunity. Still, we both had a lot to thank God for, including the timely New Hampshire rain and mud.

CHAPTER 26

Real Older Sisters

My sister, Julie, continued to ride the school bus to both junior high and high school. I just couldn't ride that bus except on bad weather days. I chose to ride my bike. It gave me a sense of freedom as did playing Little League baseball and working at my part-time jobs. And Mom wasn't expecting me to be home within one hour after school anymore.

Two of my favorite customers were older sisters who owned a dress shop in town. Their brother, a priest, inherited lots of money (so I'd heard) and left it to them when he died. They lived together in a very large two-story house situated on a corner lot with a beautifully designed wood fence around it. Their house was right out of the early 1920s–1930s era with most of their furnishings being of high quality. Also, on the back part of the property was a cottage, which they rented, and a large two-car garage with a seldom used Lincoln Zephyr parked in it. What a car!

My jobs included mowing and trimming the lawn, washing the windows, cleaning the lily pad pool, polishing the brass eagle statue on the lawn, wiping the Zephyr down, and vacuuming the whole house, all of which I really liked doing because it gave me a feeling of being part of the uniqueness of it all. In the wintertime, I cleaned the house and shoveled the front walks and driveway. I did many other special cleaning and repairing projects for them, but the one I enjoyed most was painting their cellar stairs and basement floor. Occasionally, I did some cleaning at their dress shop but not much else there. They were generous and timely payers.

Whenever they had a project for me to do, they either called me at home or at my grandmother's and left a message. Sometimes they just wanted company. They'd ask me when I could visit and what I'd like to eat. For a young farm boy, it doesn't get any better than that.

The sisters often cooked for me. I enjoyed each meal, as well as their company. They seemed to prefer eating at home rather than dealing with the hassle of going out to a restaurant. I believe it was because they really enjoyed cooking for themselves.

They liked to drink, socialize, and cook for guests. Up until that time, I hadn't had very good experiences with people drinking, but this was a completely different story. These two ladies really had the habit and were very social when they imbibed. The good news was that they usually didn't drink and cook for their guests at the same time. I was hesitant to tell my folks and grandmother about their drinking for fear they wouldn't let me work for them. The sisters were always ladies when I was around—and a load of laughs, especially when they were lit. Their funny stories had me crying from laughing so hard.

They gave me a key to the cellar door so that I could come and go when needed. Many times they'd be napping by the time I finished my work. I worked very hard to justify their investment in me. I felt as if I were part of their family—not in the 1950s but, rather, what I imagined it would have been like in the roaring 20s. At times, it was like a fantasy.

One day, I got a call that they wanted me to come down and clean up their kitchen. They said that there'd been an accident and I needed to get there as soon as possible. When I walked into the kitchen, I couldn't believe my eyes. It seems that they had been cooking and drinking and somehow started a fire. The fire had been so bad that it burned a big hole in the ceiling and all the way up through the roof. They wanted me to clean up as much as I could so they'd be able to use part of the kitchen until the contractors had time to reconstruct it. I smiled inside but knew this was serious. I worked a few hours and went home a black, sooty mess.

The last time that I spent any time there was after one of the sisters fell down the cellar stairs. I hoped it wasn't my paint job. She had seriously hurt herself, although she said she didn't feel any pain. From then on, they had a full-time caretaker and booze guard in the house. Therefore, they didn't need much help from me.

CHAPTER 27

Moving Up

Being an eighth grader in the same building with high school students had its advantages, as long as you weren't easily intimidated. Within less than a year, if my grades were up to par, I'd move into high school and not be restricted to specific parts of the building anymore. I'd also be able to spend more time in the school library staying up-to-date on current events.

I knew I'd eventually be associated with one of the many clicks in high school, which seemed important to some of my classmates. I could be tagged as a Future Farmer of America, auto-shop guy, jock, cheerleader, class officer, intellectual, band member, smoker, or one not worth tagging. Kids can be cruel sometimes, but like adults, they seem to be more comfortable when everyone around them has an invisible label.

I ended up with no tag my freshman year and then "jock" for the rest of my high school years. It wasn't bad because I was identified with a winning team manned by a few very bright students.

The additional tag of "Canuck" stuck with me and other students whose parents or grandparents came from Canada and spoke French as their first language. My dad and Pepére spoke French much of the time, which was fine. Both had served in the US Army and earned their chips, so I was proud of being of Canadian descent.

To me, the key to not being intimidated in high school was accepting the labels you were given and leveraging them when they worked to your advantage. I had no problem being perceived as a Frenchman. Everyone knew Frenchmen grew up to be good lovers, so what was there to worry about? I preferred being tagged as a jock rather than as a smoker or one not worth tagging. Most of the tagging was subtle and not intentionally painful. I realized that moving up to a better tag had nothing to do with your social class and everything to do with your age and grades.

The Scriptures teach that having a good reputation is important, and I believed it was more important than being financially liquid. I found that many times my reputation helped me in high school and in ways I never expected.

One day, a very smart guy from the next class up stopped me in the hallway and asked me if I'd be interested in taking his paper route for him while he and his family went on vacation.

I asked, "Steinberg, why me?"

He said, "Everyone knows you can be trusted and that you work very hard." That made my day. I thought for a few minutes, as he continued talking, that he was pulling my chain and then decided, what difference did it make? I liked him and this was not about me. His family owned the junkyard where I hid one evening when I was in elementary school.

Steinberg invited me over to his house and laid out his plan. I'd work his route for a month, and when he returned he'd take it back. I'd keep all of the money I earned while he was gone.

He walked me through all of the steps from picking up the papers at the store each morning to collecting money for them at week's end. We set a day for me to walk the route with him early in the morning. Then we shook hands, and I cleared all of it with Mom when I got home that night.

I enjoyed the new experience of delivering the papers on my bike and collecting for them at the end of the week. I was working in someone else's world, and I was motivated to leave it in as good or better shape than it was given to me. I was very careful to follow the notes that I'd written in my new address book during the instructional run we'd done together.

The first week's collections were a pleasant surprise. I received a lot of tips. He hadn't mentioned tips. Had he wanted to surprise me or had he just not thought of them? I wasn't sure. Did he receive tips? I was sure he did.

One week, after I finished collecting money from the customers, I ended up near a small grocery store on Portland Street. I rewarded myself with a dozen sugared doughnuts and a quart of cold Orange Crush. I thought, *What are tips for if not for splurging occasionally?*

When Steinberg returned from vacation, I handed him back his bag and suggested he call me again when he took another vacation. From that point on, we became somewhat closer—not buddies or friends, just more familiar with each other. I liked it. It felt as though we were business associates, and trusted ones at that.

One of the side benefits of helping him was having my new address book. I added other friends' and family members' addresses and phone numbers to it and kept it up-to-date. Later, it became the key to securing a critically needed job at the right time.

Making Stuff

I was encouraged as I watched other junior high school students succeed. Some classes were quite large while other classes were quite small. I truly enjoyed the smaller-sized classes, especially when the subjects were complex. It was good to get to know other students and listen to them as they found ways to learn complex new ideas.

For the first time, I was spending time with fellow students who seemed to know where they were going in life. They had a plan. Each course they took and each grade they received counted. Most of the girls were more verbal than the boys and appeared to be more comfortable in language classes.

Attending junior high school in a portion of the high school building was unique. Even though the older students owned the campus, they were nice to us most of the time. It was exciting for me to observe a number of the upperclassmen driving beautiful cars back and forth to school. Some of the cars were customized and usually parked outside the school auto shop. As time passed, I learned that some of those students worked after school and on weekends to pay for the luxury of owning their own cars. This was a whole new world to me, and I was determined to learn more about it.

I questioned some of the older students and found out that when I turned fourteen I could get a work permit. The permit process required the approval of the superintendent of schools. That was one more reason not to get into too much trouble and limit my opportunities.

I dreamed of finding a part-time job that could support having a car in high school. I had no idea what I'd do because I didn't have any special work skills. I did come to realize that doing something stupid could potentially restrict my work opportunities later on, so most of the time I cooled it.

Now back to the real world—focus, focus. For now, I needed to be content with biking. I tried not being envious of smarter students and guys driving cars, but I had to remind myself that I was only human. My daydreams were about how much fun I'd have driving back and forth to school. I felt it would be the next step to more freedom, or maybe it was just the itch to grow up. I learned not to scratch that itch, along with a few others that were developing.

—◊—

Even though my brother, Monty, was ten years younger than I, we always had fun together. He'd climb up and sit in my lap facing me and we'd play our slap game. It started off by him softly slapping me on the cheek. I softly slapped him back. He slapped me again, not so softly. I slapped him back again, not so softly. When we weren't slapping we kept our hands to our sides. We laughed as each anticipated the next slap. This went on for a while. Eventually, he'd either end up on the floor or Mom would run into the room and tell us to stop. He and I did lots of things together and most of them included some wrestling and laughing. My sisters and I were close but not as physical as Monty and me.

My new bike gave me a great deal of freedom but didn't do much for Monty. We decided to build a bike trailer so that he'd be able to come along with me on some of my trips. Together, we worked on the project in the garage—our clubhouse.

We found some large-spoke wheels and an axle from off an old carriage. By using the wood stored in the basement and garage, we were able to build a box-like trailer with sides high enough for him to sit in and hold on to the top rails. The biggest challenge we encountered was how to connect the trailer to the bike. Wood alone was unsafe, and steel alone was almost impossible to work with. We finally found a six-foot piece of metal about two inches wide and a quarter inch thick. We bent it around the tire and cut a two-by-ten in a half circle and bolted it under the bent metal bar to keep it sturdy. It worked just fine.

Monty and I traveled around town together and visited our relatives. He had to put a pillow on the floor of the trailer to sit on because the ride was so rough, but he didn't complain. Mom put restrictions on where I could take him, so our adventures were limited. He eventually got his own bike with training wheels. By then, he'd grown too big for the bike trailer anyway.

—⁓—

I thought about my bedroom. I was tired of walking on an attic floor that wasn't nailed down. The boards were rough because they had never been run through a planer. There was insulation and two-by-eight cross members under the boards. I felt that the rough boards were just the base flooring and that later, when the upstairs was finished, we could nail down finished flooring or plywood and all would be fine. Mom agreed, but there were no comments from Dad about his thoughts on the subject.

When Dad was at work, I started nailing the floor down by using some of the old nails from the torn down shed—those that weren't too rusty. Mom encouraged me to nail down only the boards in the area where I was sleeping. I was learning that there was something uniquely exciting about improving your own nest.

The attic was a great place to sleep; it was totally open. My bed was set up on the back side of the house near the window. From the window, I looked out over the backyard and all the way to the woods. When deer walked through the back fields, I sat on my bed and watched them.

Lying in bed, I could easily see over to the other side of the attic and the chimney that went from the floor to the roof. Its bricks made it look like a King Arthur tower. When the evening light faded, I went off to sleep but often woke up a few hours later. The light from the streetlight flickered through the side window and created shadows that looked like someone or something was climbing up the chimney bricks. Being a bit frightened, I ducked my head under the covers and went back to sleep.

Some nights the sound of heavy rain on the roof was deafening because there was no insulation in the ceiling, and flashes of lightning made the attic seem huge. Those nights taught me not to fear bad weather. In fact, as long as I wasn't outside when it was lightning, I loved the rain.

My space in the attic was pretty bare except for the bed, dresser, and desk; so I decided to make a lamp and a desk cabinet for the top of my desk to hold all of my stationery, pens, supplies, and stuff.

One of the positives of having the junior high school in the same building as the high school was that we seventh and eighth graders could attend shop classes. There was a wood shop and an auto shop. Both shops added a new dimension to many of the students' studies because learning a trade was critical to them. When they reached the age of sixteen, they'd have no choice but to go to work to help support their families.

In addition to my shop class, designing a lamp for my bedroom meant visiting furniture stores. I wanted to make something different—bright but also soft. My desk wasn't small, but I decided that the base of the lamp couldn't be larger than a foot in diameter. I wanted it to be tall enough to spread light over the entire desk and most of my nailed-down sleeping area.

I decided on a lamp made of polished wood and deep-green plastic. I visualized that the plastic would reflect light at night and the polished wood would soften the reflection. I searched through the school shop inventory of wood and plastic, but there wasn't much to choose from. Finally, I found some plastic at the hardware store and two small pieces of finished maple in the wood rack under our basement stairs. Using cardboard from an empty box, I cut different sized circles until I found the right combination.

With a small hand jigsaw, I started cutting a circular maple lamp base. I sanded it until it was an almost perfect circle—careful not to round the edges. I cut six smaller maple circles for the lamp tower. Each circle had to match the others perfectly. I varnished each piece, sanded the varnish smooth with light sandpaper, and varnished them again until they all had that soft, finished look.

Afterwards, I cut matching plastic circles for each piece of maple that I had cut. The plastic had adhesive paper protecting it from scratching. The challenge was to perfectly sand and polish the tower edges so that the plastic circles would be half an inch larger than the wood circles they would separate. Together, they needed to look as if they came from a professional factory and made that way.

Most of the work on the lamp was done in the garage while I listened to beautiful background music on the radio. I used some of Dad's tools, but drilling a hole through the center of each piece required a power drill, so I got permission from the junior high shop teacher to use the drill. I ran a half-inch steel nipple through the holes and bolted all of the circles together at the top and bottom.

Western Auto had the electrical parts I needed and four little risers to tack to the bottom of the lamp to lift it off the table and make room for the cord. After I found a nice shade for it at the five-and-ten-cents store, the lamp was finished. The deep-green plastic reflected the light. The maple had a warm glow and the wood grain added character. I liked it!

The shop teacher suggested we place the lamp in the Rochester Fair—where it received an A award. He then suggested we send it to Ford Motor Company and let it compete with other projects in Ford's national contest. A few months later, the lamp came home with a nice letter from Ford and a check for twenty dollars. Not bad, considering the price of gas at that time was twenty-nine cents a gallon. I was encouraged to do more.

My mother also wanted me to keep busy. She'd say, "Idle hands are the devil's handiwork."

—m—

Most of the cash I earned while attending junior high school came from mowing lawns, shoveling snow, and helping older women clean their homes. I enjoyed the work and the wonderful way each of my customers treated me. But it was impossible to find the kind of work that would generate the level of cash I really needed for my projects.

One day, Pepére suggested I talk to his Greek friend, who owned a restaurant in the center of town, about helping him on his vegetable truck farm. If you were under the age of fourteen, you could work on farms, homes, and in restaurants, but not many other places. I knew the government was trying to protect me from being forced to work, but I wasn't happy about it.

Pepére invited me to supper at the restaurant. Whenever he wanted to take me out to eat, I always felt complimented. He picked me up at home, and when we got to the restaurant, we sat at a booth near the windows. Pepére and I shared one of his favorite Greek dishes, and we ate lots of bread. While we were eating, the owner stopped by, sat down, and introduced himself to me.

He said he had three to four days' worth of weeding that needed to be done in his vegetable garden at his small farm on Rochester Hill Road, and he asked if I'd be interested in doing it. I was interested. I looked him straight in the eyes and inquired, "How much are you paying?"

Looking straight back at me, he replied, "Forty dollars for the entire job. How good are you at weeding?"

I described what I had done at home, for my grandmother, and others. Impressed, he said, "It sounds like you'll have no problem with my weeds."

I biked to his farm the next morning and, as we had agreed, he arrived shortly after seven o'clock. I started right off. He stayed for a while and watched me closely. Then he left to run some errands, saying that he would be back later.

It was late spring and the days were longer, so I was able to finish all the weeding before dark that first day. I biked home with my light on and biked back again early in the morning to pick up my pay. He was there when I arrived, and we walked the garden together.

He said, "Good job," and handed me fifteen dollars.

I said, "The deal was forty dollars."

He said, "Take the fifteen dollars or leave it; it is up to you kid."

I was not happy. I took the fifteen dollars and biked down to see Pepére about his friend. He said he was sorry and would talk to him for me. A few days later, Pepére informed me that the Greek wouldn't budge. This was the first time I had been shortchanged—and by my grandfather's friend. I didn't understand why Pepére let his buddy cheat me out of twenty-five dollars.

My first lesson from this experience was related to the relationship I had with Pepére. His friends didn't call him the French Jew for nothing, I learned. From that day forward, when it came to work and money, I stayed away from Pepére. The second lesson related to working for strangers. I decided to become more selective. I stayed on a pay-as-you-go basis. For every day I worked, I got paid for that day, in cash. Grandpa had a saying: I work for pay and not for fun. I want my pay when my work is done.

No more cash at the end of projects for strangers. It took me a couple of weeks to think this through thoroughly, and what I came up with was that it was partly my fault. I didn't take into account that he most likely thought it was a big job; therefore, he was willing to pay forty dollars. Unintentionally, I may have embarrassed him by doing it in one day. I was finding out that hard work doesn't always get rewarded. I needed to get smarter in negotiating jobs in the future.

—⁓—

I purchased some cherry wood with the fifteen dollars. It was for my new desktop cabinet that I was going to make. I had seen a picture of one in a magazine and drew out the detailed plans for it on a paper shopping bag.

Cherry wood is a very hard wood, and when polished it is beautiful. The cabinet was designed to be about two feet long and have three shelves in the center with cabinets on each side. I don't remember any other wood being that tough to work with. I attached the doors on each cabinet with small brass hinges and brass screws. I ruined half a dozen brass screws trying to attach the hinges to the cabinet and the cabinet doors.

When completed, the cabinet had a fantastic shine and also won an A award at the Rochester Fair. The wood was a light color with beautiful red grains running through it. In some places, it looked as if it were softly and slowly bleeding.

While working on the cabinet in the garage, I thought a lot about the Greek and wondered how a restaurant owner could be so stupid. What a privilege to own and run a successful restaurant in a small town in New Hampshire. If he shortchanged me, I'm sure he shorted lots of others. Should the word get around, it wouldn't help his business. Who'd want that kind of reputation? I felt a little sorry for Pepére for he loved Greek food, and that was the only Greek restaurant around.

I had made too many things for myself; therefore, I was thinking it was time to do something for my family. I wanted to build my dad a boat and my mom a vanity for her bedroom wall. I had enjoyed working with plastic while making my lamp, so I thought, *Why not make the vanity out of plastic and metal?* It wasn't going to be a large vanity, because she wasn't a woman with lots of perfume or makeup. I decided that it would have dark-red plastic shelves with scalloped black metal brackets holding up the shelves.

It was a fun project, but I found that working with metal was much harder than plastic and wood. When it was finished, the shop teacher again suggested that we enter it in the Rochester Fair. It didn't do as well as the lamp and cabinet had, but Mom loved it—and that's what mattered most.

—⁓—

Pepére had a nice boat and car, but my dad had neither. That didn't seem right to me. So one day, while sitting down across from Dad in the dining room, I asked, "Dad, would you let me build you a boat?"

His response was, "Kids don't build boats!"

"Are you sure you don't want me to build you a boat? I'd love to, Dad!"

"Didn't you hear me? Kids don't build boats!"

"So, are you okay if I build one for myself then?"

"Go to it!" Then he chuckled and said, "Kids!"

Monty's bike trailer

CHAPTER 29

An Unnatural Fit

There are times when you know exactly what to do and then there are times when you are clueless. I'd been playing the trombone since I was in third grade. Now I was in the junior high school band and looking forward to playing in the high school marching band. No one else in my immediate family played any musical instruments.

As I looked forward to high school, I reflected on comments my dad had made about his freshman year when he was the kicker on the varsity football team. Whenever he shared his experiences, he almost always ended his stories by telling us the one about someone stealing his good football shoes just before the final game of the year. He said it was impossible to kick with the oversized replacement shoes he'd been given—and you know the rest of the story. His team lost the game. He didn't continue playing high school football because he left school to marry my mom and work full-time.

I wasn't playing junior high football and nobody noticed. Dad's football experience was on my mind, and I shared my thoughts with my mom. When it came to making decisions, she'd say, "Jacob, you will make the right decision."

I never understood her response. She listened and moved her head up and down, and I guess I continued to hope she'd suggest a direction. Mom seemed to think I knew what I was doing—little did she know. At times, I believed she had her own opinion but for some reason wouldn't voice it.

Maybe she wanted me to gain the ability to make good decisions myself. And the only way to do that was to let me make them without her input and either enjoy the benefits of a good decision or learn from bad ones.

As much as I loved music, playing the trombone didn't come natural to me. When I was in grammar school, a guy picked a fight with me after school primarily because he hated listening to me practice while he was in detention. Over the years I improved some, but you didn't have to play at a very high level to get into the junior high school band. It was a small school and they needed everyone they could find.

Making decisions was not new to me, but I hated stupidity and making mistakes. Now that I was getting older, I felt that making the right decision was more critical because with some decisions there's no way back. I thought about my folks' often-verbalized regrets on decisions they'd made when they were young.

During my junior-high years, I became physically stronger and faster. I had experienced some success playing baseball in both Little League and the VFW League and felt there was a chance I could play football as well as most guys my age.

I was also too poor not to think through any decision that would involve money. I was most content when I was getting paid for physical work. The decision process relating to work and getting paid was by now pretty basic. It was simple: if I wanted freedom, I had to earn it. I was convinced that playing the trombone would never make me rich. I'd get my letters for contributing to the band, but in the long run there would be no college scholarship for me in music.

It was too early to tell, but there was a strong possibility that I could end up playing pretty good football based on my baseball experience and my improved physical strength and speed. Dad was very athletic and Mom was quite strong, so there was a better than 50 percent chance of me being at least a good football player.

Some of the guys in our class were talking about leaving school to go to work when they turned fourteen. They already had work permits and knew what they wanted to do for work the rest of their lives. One guy specifically loved to work on cars and spent all of his extra time either in the school auto shop or working in an auto shop in town.

It bugged me that my dad had quit school and hadn't gone back to school after serving in the army. Not taking advantage of the G.I. Bill limited his earnings and made it financially tough on him and Mom. I didn't judge him for his decision, but at the same time I didn't want my earning power to be limited.

High-paying jobs were almost defined as jobs requiring a college education. I knew my family was not in a financial position to pay for that. I'd have to find funds from other sources. It was way too early to tell, but maybe playing football was the answer.

All of this thinking about the future was important, but something was troubling me and I couldn't ignore it. I hated it when I didn't do something very well. If I couldn't be the best at something, or close to the best with a chance to improve, I found it upsetting. I don't know what to call it, but an inner voice was saying to me: *You are mediocre at playing a musical instrument*; so after five years of trying, it's time to play the radio instead. I'm not sure that it wasn't the Holy Spirit leading me, because I prayed about it enough.

In the end, I didn't give up music for football. I walked away from it because I wasn't excellent at it. There is only so much time in a day, and because being excellent at something made me feel better, I decided to stop wasting my time on the trombone. I was learning that sometimes you just have to walk away.

The same thought process applied to dating girls. If I couldn't do it in style, I wasn't going to do it. I knew many nice girls, but I was broke and not interested in settling for second best. Dating would have to come later. In addition, I noticed that some smart and good-looking girls were riding around school in cars driven by older guys. It seemed logical to me that if two guys had the same potential and were equal in most other respects, a smart girl would pick the guy with the car. What girl wanted to walk?

I did become more attracted to girls while in junior high school, but I didn't want to get physically involved. I hadn't forgotten the beautiful young girl walking in Seth Richards's neighborhood a few years back who had become pregnant at a very young age. I had also not forgotten watching two dogs near the grammar school, and they were stuck together for the longest time. The mechanics of lovemaking weren't familiar to me, but the last thing I wanted was for that to happen to me.

CHAPTER 30

Skipper's Beginning

I quickly realized that selecting the high school classes I needed to take involved more than a casual attitude of "I'll take whatever everyone else is taking." The selection process was paramount to forecasting what group I'd be in and how I'd earn a living for the rest of my life.

Depending upon my choices, I'd either be taking college prep courses or not. It was one of the toughest periods of my teenage years. For some, they planned to learn a trade and then leave school. Other students took college-prep courses because their families had very specific professional plans for them. Many students took college-prep courses hoping that in the future they'd find a way to fund college. I was one of those students.

Since my immediate family worked in the woolen mills, they were considered trades people. The industry was in the middle of an enormous change with the strength of the unions growing. Management and unions were involved in a never-ending battle over hourly wages and benefits. Very cheap foreign labor was available overseas, and it appeared that it wouldn't be long before the owners of the mills moved much of their manufacturing out of the United States. This was not good for either our town or for the New England area.

The Portsmouth Naval Shipyard, which was about twenty-five miles from home, was cutting back now that the war was over. It was impossible to predict when the economy would pick up, considering much of the economy had historically been tied to war production. Southern New

Hampshire was caught between a rock and a hard place. Few new industries were moving in and many were ready to move overseas.

Drafting was a freshman class and naturally followed junior high shop classes. Surprisingly, drafting was considered a college preparation class, so I signed up for that along with all of the normal college-prep classes. But drafting was special because I wanted to build a boat.

I was excited about designing a boat that would be both fast and good looking. Dad had refused my offer to build him a boat. His response was not surprising when I remembered that he wanted me to enjoy my youth. I knew I couldn't do it alone, and I didn't want to do it just for myself. Although Dad had freed me from making anything for him, he unintentionally committed me to building something we could all enjoy and be proud of.

Our family had serious financial limitations, and I was determined to not let this project make things worse. There were more job opportunities on the horizon for me as I got older, so I was optimistic that over time I'd be able to fund all of the costs.

I was fairly good at designing and building small, simple things. Because of this, I felt that the drafting class would give me a good opportunity to begin the boat building process.

Teenage life was not simple. Everything you did or didn't do seemed to have some long-term ramification. My advanced math and drafting courses made me think about becoming a mechanical engineer. I didn't know any mechanical engineers, but I did have an uncle who was an electrical engineer. He was challenged and did well financially.

The drafting class was fun and productive. The tools were easy to use, and the projects were creative and very detailed. In addition to the basic class tasks, we had to select a unique project of our own. Drafting the plans for my boat was the only project I could think about, and I hoped the teacher would approve it as a qualified project for class credit.

When I think of the place I liked best in our beautiful high school, I think of the library for it allowed me access to books and periodicals—and it was a great social place. It had conference rooms and a pleasant second-story view. I preferred to sit at a table near the window and feel the sun while I read an interesting periodical, like *Popular Mechanics*. It was full of stories about things people had built. I read every *Popular Mechanics* magazine that the library had.

In one edition, I came across a story about a man who had built a twelve-foot, Class B racing boat. He had designed it himself; I thought it was the kind of boat I'd enjoy. It had a front seat large enough for two people and kneeling pads and foot holes for the driver in the rear. It looked like a combination racing and fun boat.

I showed the article to the drafting teacher and asked if enlarging the plans in the article to usable blueprint size would satisfy the special project class requirements. I also shared that I planned to build the boat. He said, "Yes," but gave me that disbelieving look.

The drawings in the magazine were very small and detailed. The scale was quite simple, but I needed to cut the pages out of the magazine and lay each one flat before converting them to larger patterns. I couldn't use the school's copy, so I checked out all of the stores and found a copy to buy for myself. There was no blueprint equipment in the high school, so I went to the stationery store and found the appropriate paper for the full-blown pattern. I completed the drawings and submitted them for credit. They were approved, and I ended up with a good grade on them.

The patterns needed to be enlarged again to actual production size, but I couldn't find the correct paper for this. I improvised by cutting up paper grocery bags and taping them together. It was exciting to create the patterns of the stern, bulkhead, and steering wheel support beam of the boat. Each of the items was a key part of the frame of the boat. They would be attached to the oak strips that would run horizontally from the stem to the stern of the boat.

The practical use of drafting techniques made me feel comfortable about the first stages of building the boat. I knew in my soul that I'd build it. I shared the patterns with the drafting teacher, and he laughed at my paper-bag patterns. Later I found out that this was the easy part of the building process.

One of the toughest parts of this project would be finding the money to fund it. I had no idea what the total cost of the boat and motor would be. The initial steps in building it required oak for the frame that would hold the waterproof plywood outer shell tightly together. There couldn't be any knots in the oak, and it would have to be steamed and bent to form the hull of the boat. I'd use mahogany frames to hold the oak strips. The mahogany couldn't have any weak points or knots of any kind in it.

I took my bike and shopped around at the local building supply stores, but none had what I needed. A clerk at one of the stores suggested a store in Sanford, Maine. That was too far away to go on my bike, so I made a call and obtained a quote. It was a lot of money.

—∞—

We burned coal and wood for winter heat, whichever was cheaper. We had a coal bin in our basement and either coal or wood was shoveled or tossed through an opened basement window onto a metal chute. Both made lots of noise as they slid down the chute into the basement.

Many years before, a hurricane hit our part of New England. It was easy for me to remember the hurricane because we still had some elm tree mementoes on the side lawn. As a result of the hurricane, many of the streets in town were blocked by huge fallen elms.

My dad borrowed Uncle Ted's car and trailer and hauled home cut sections of the elm trees. He rolled the sections off the trailer and lined them up beside our house in three straight rows that ran the length of the house. His plan was to use them as firewood once they dried out. Each piece was about three feet in diameter and two and a half feet thick. Dad worked very hard getting them home. I remember standing in the trailer while he rolled the sections onto it and again later as he rolled them off the trailer.

I asked Mom how much a winter's supply of wood or coal for the furnace cost. She said a lot and asked why I was interested. I suggested that I split the elm so that they wouldn't have to order any coal or wood for winter. She said that Dad had already tried and found that the elm was almost impossible to split. So I asked if she'd approach Dad with the idea when he got home. They could pay me what they felt was a reasonable amount for splitting and stacking the wood in the basement. That way, we'd both win.

I was delighted that Dad was agreeable to my offer. He said, "If you can split and stack the wood in the basement, I'll drive you to Sanford, Maine to get the materials you need to build the boat."

I hoped he was saying this because he believed I could do it and also because it would save them some money. But you never know, right? I took it as a show of confidence because I wanted to believe him. Dad knew I had split a lot of wood for my grandparents, and I'm sure he was hopeful I could do it because times were tough, and it would save him some money. At the same time, I'm remembering his words that "kids don't build boats!"

Surely, he was reminded daily of the unfinished elm project sitting beside the house and wanted that off his to-do list. We had a lot going for us on this project, and in my heart I wasn't going to let them or myself down. I was truly motivated.

Our basement floor was basic dirt with the exception of the cement under the coal bin, the boiler, and the cold-storage area. A bulkhead with stairs giving us access to the basement was situated on the back side of the house. The dimensions of the bulkhead and the door were critical to me because I wanted to frame the boat in the basement and then move it into the garage when the framing was completed. I also planned to carry the split elm down through the bulkhead and into the basement and then stack it along the wall in front of the coal bin.

The splitting process started with a broken axe handle. I learned that elm doesn't split with axes. It takes a sledge hammer with iron splitting wedges or a splitting axe. We had the wedges and the sledge hammer and a small axe for finishing the split.

As the days passed, I gained strength and confidence and learned a lot about the grain of elm trees and how to use the grain to my advantage. I developed some calluses on both hands, but my gloves prevented blistering. It's hard to swing a sledge hammer accurately when you are exhausted, so I paced my work and learned not to work when I was too tired.

I enjoyed splitting in the freshness of the morning air before the sun got high in the sky. I also enjoyed it when it was hot. I just slowed down and drank lots of cold water. When I got hungry, I stopped and walked out to the garden and pulled some carrots. After I washed them off under the faucet, I ate them to my heart's content. There was something wonderful about working hard in the sun as long as I didn't have to do it for a living.

I wore shirts with long sleeves when I toted the split elm into the basement. Many weeks passed before all of the elm wood was split and stored. It looked great stacked tall against the basement wall. The stacks went the full length of the wall. All of the chips were in bushel baskets to be used for kindling. The house looked taller without the elm sitting next to it, and the newly expanded lawn looked great. The split elm smelled delightful and gave the basement a fresh woodsy smell.

Dad asked when I wanted to go to Sanford for the oak and mahogany. I told him I needed to get a firm quote and then we could plan the trip. He was ready and I was delighted. Mom made a special supper celebrating the finished project, and we all had a fun Saturday night playing games. The boat building process was in sight, and I was overjoyed.

CHAPTER 31

Cadet Rocky

Membership in formal organizations was not new to me. I'd already been in Sunday school and church, Cub Scouts, Boy Scouts, Little League, V F.W baseball, and now Civil Air Patrol. Each organization fostered loyalty to family and country, self-reliance, self-discipline, and the development of social and problem-solving skills. Each also brought new information with it, but no organization gave me as much insight into the outside world as the Civil Air Patrol did.

Once or twice a month, depending upon the subject material we were focused on, we cadets met at the National Guard Armory on the other side of town. Our local civil air patrol unit was small, and we didn't have convenient access to planes. But one year, we, along with other cadets throughout the state, had an opportunity to take a trip to visit Loring Air Force Base in Limestone, Maine (Aroostook County). We were all loaded into a two-engine plane and flown to the base. Loring was a Strategic Air Command (SAC) base with state-of-the-art equipment and facilities.

Most of our time spent at the base was focused on the air force and its mission. We visited the control tower, got to look inside some planes, and attended classes. The air force personnel came from all over the country. They shared with us a little of what they did. For those interested in a career in the United States Air Force, this was an excellent way to begin researching specific jobs and their requirements.

We'd been encouraged to pack some clothes for physical training. I took sneakers, shorts, and a comfortable tee shirt. However, no formal physical training classes had been scheduled for us. My high school had a wonderful gymnasium with locker rooms, shower facilities, and offices for the coaches. Therefore, I was interested in seeing what the air force personnel had for training facilities, and I hoped to be able to use them. So one day after our classes were finished, I found the gymnasium, which was just a short distance from where we were housed.

Their facility was huge. Dressed in casual clothes, I walked inside toting my small bag of personal items. Some guys were playing basketball and others were using the exercise machines. Two healthy-looking guys wearing small, thin boxing gloves were at the punching bags. One seemed to be about my height and the other was at least eight inches taller than I was. I noticed an elevated boxing ring adjacent to the workout area. I'd never seen a real boxing ring before, so I walked over and checked it out.

The two fellows working the punching bags came over and introduced themselves. They asked what my name was, where I was from, and if I had just been assigned to the base. I explained that I was not assigned to the base but was a guest and part of the civil air patrol unit. We're just visiting for a few days.

They both welcomed me and asked if I wanted to work out. I told them that I was hoping to be able to. The taller one asked if I'd ever boxed before. When I said that I had, but just a little, he asked if I'd be interested in boxing a few rounds.

I smelled someone wanting fresh blood. So I carefully answered by asking, "Who with?"

He said, "Either one of us; take your pick."

I looked closely and then pointed to the shorter guy, thinking that the taller guy's reach had to be ten inches more than mine.

They showed me to the locker room and instructed me to pick a locker. I was assured that no one would touch my stuff. They left me there to change clothes while the shorter guy went to find me some gloves and a head protector.

It appeared that I was going to get all the exercise I wanted and maybe more. I'd been looking for exercise, not a fight. Somehow, it seemed that things like that kept happening to me no matter where I went.

As I changed into my shorts and tee shirt, I thought about the few fights I'd had and the lessons my dad taught me. I also recalled the week I'd spent at summer camp a few years earlier. As a gift, my grandmother paid for each of her nineteen grandchildren to attend a Christian camp one time for one week during the summer. The boys' camp was located in Plymouth, New Hampshire.

My thoughts quickly focused back on "conflict night," which was held every Wednesday. Anyone in the camp could challenge anyone else to enter the boxing ring to resolve a conflict. No one had to participate; it was totally voluntary.

For some reason, one of my Christian brothers was unhappy with me and wanted me in the ring with him. I remember exchanging words with him. I'm sure I had made some smart remark, and he figured that this was his chance to get even. We were the same size. I didn't know how to walk away, so I didn't.

The boxing gloves we used were huge. They were like large, heavy couch pillows. I could understand why they weren't worried about anyone getting hurt. He was very much "in my face" all during the fight. His hands and feet were always moving. I don't believe I'd ever seen anyone so busy—he tired me out. Like my dad had suggested, I waited and threw a few jabs to keep him away, and then I hit him hard with my left and quickly followed with a right cross. It startled him for a bit, but he quickly recovered and started his busy routine again.

This is the way it went for three rounds. By then it was obvious that we had both had enough. I would say it was about even at the end of the third round, and I wasn't interested in overtime. The gloves won—they were so heavy. After the counselor made sure we were okay, he took off our gloves and we shook hands. We were the best of buddies for the rest of the week. Lessons learned.

Important to the fight-at-hand with a member of the US Air Force was the memory of not having been able to knock down my summer-camp opponent and end the fight when I had wanted to. I didn't know these air force guys, so I felt that I needed to be sharper than ever before if I hoped to end it with a victory.

As I walked out, I noticed that a few people were gathered around the ring. The basketball game was over, and I saw that two other visiting cadets had found their way to the gymnasium. I pulled the gloves on. They were nicely padded and not too heavy. The tall, smiling boxer helped me slip my head protector on. Then he tightly tied the strings of the head protector and my gloves. When I climbed into the ring, it felt larger than I had remembered it to be just a few minutes before. It was not solid like a floor. There was some spring to it—hence the reference to canvas.

My opponent had a mouthpiece and was dancing up and down across the ring. I didn't know how to dance and didn't have a mouthpiece, so I just waited for a bell. There was none. But soon a large fellow wearing a sweatshirt climbed into the ring and motioned for us to come to the center of the ring. He was the referee. He said, "Three rounds or a knockout, whichever comes first; on my whistle."

The first round went pretty well. My opponent was a good boxer and moved around a lot. He jabbed with his left and set me up several times for a right cross but had a hard time delivering with the power he hoped to. I didn't deliver powerful punches with my right, but I did with my left.

The second round was more intense. I became really focused; I saw nothing but him. He was very quick and busy like my summer-camp friend. I hit him hard with three left jabs and just as I was throwing a right, someone called his name and he turned to look. His jaw was unprotected. He dropped to the floor. I stepped back and said to myself, *Not good, but please don't get up right away!*

Slowly he got to his feet and then charged at me. He was mad and I knew why. I wasn't mad and knew I needed to be or otherwise I was going to be seriously hurt.

He didn't know it, but I was fourteen and to serve in the air force he had to be at least eighteen. That day, and at that moment, age made no difference. He hit me pretty hard on my arms and shoulders. I was glad I had the head protector on or my ears would have been more than red. If I ended up with a cauliflower ear, my mother would be really upset.

I realized that he was trying hard to push me to the floor, but I had pretty good balance. Half a dozen times I hit him in the abdomen as hard as I could in an effort to make him stop. He backed off a little. The whistle blew and ended round two.

The tall boxer was in his corner talking to him, and he wasn't smiling anymore. I looked down and there was blood on the canvas—it was mine.

My nose was bleeding again, but this wasn't grammar school—no one cared. In spite of the nose, I could breathe okay and felt strong. I wasn't as tired as I thought I might be at this point in the fight. Hopefully my stamina would last. I realized that I was finally where I needed to be emotionally.

The whistle blew for the last round. As the round progressed, I could sense that he was trying to knock me out as he went for my head every other punch. His swings to my head gave me clearer shots to his body. It had been his buddy who screamed at him. I hadn't, but I was fighting for more than my exercise now and knew it. Still, the hardest thing was to wait and hold back for the right time to throw the correct punch because he never stopped swinging at my head. I thought I heard noises like a truck coming or driving by, or maybe it just was my imagination. His head protector was in my face much of the time, so I couldn't see where the noise was coming from. The whistle. I heard it—or did I?

It was finally over! We looked at each other for a second. It didn't appear that we were going to be friends. He turned away. I did the same and climbed out of the ring. Someone slapped me on the shoulder and said, "Good job."

I walked to the locker room to find my clothes. For a moment, I forgot where I had put them. I cleaned my nose, washed my face, grabbed my stuff from the locker, and changed clothes. I was sweaty, but I didn't want to shower because there with strangers all around. I walked back through the boxing area and a couple more people remarked, "Nice work" and "Good show." As I headed for the door, I noticed that the two cadets had already left.

Once back in the room, I showered and took a good look at myself in the mirror. The head protector had done its job. My ears hadn't changed shape. My face was red but not cut or bruised. On the other hand, the front of my whole upper body, including my shoulders, was red and bruised, but not cut.

—⁂—

I wasn't very hungry, which was really unusual considering I'd had a very good workout. Nevertheless, I went to the dining room. There were only a few people eating. I noticed that Della Moore, a fellow cadet, was there. I had met and chatted with her earlier and learned that she was from Manchester. She was fifteen, a year older than I, and had already determined she was not joining the air force.

Seeing that she was sitting alone, I took my tray and walked over to her table and asked if she wanted company. She nodded her head yes. There were a few chairs around the circular table, and I selected the one next to her. Della moved over a little just to make more room for my tray. She asked if I had enjoyed my exercise at the gym. I blushed and told her it had been challenging. She laughed.

Something attracted me to her, but I didn't know what it was. It wasn't her beauty, although she was nice looking. With her large eyes and dark hair pinned back a little, her face and neck were accentuated. It was easy to envision her in an expensive evening gown. She had the look. Della was attractive but not in a sensual way. Okay, I lied.

She talked about her family and her church and her involvement in helping at the church after school. We were comfortable sharing and she seemed to have a peaceful nature. I knew we could be really good friends if we wanted to be.

After supper and talking with Della, I headed back to my room and slept like a baby. The next morning, I didn't have any black eyes or cauliflower ears, but I was sore and had a lot of black-and-blue marks on my arms and body.

For the next two days, I spent more time watching Della from a distance than I should have. Accidentally, we sat next to each other on the plane ride home. During the flight, she said she had made the decision to become a nun. Her older sister had become a nun three years before. Della loved helping others and intended to serve Christ in that capacity for the rest of her life. Now I knew what drew me to her. There was no doubt that meeting her was the best part of my trip.

Most of us felt that we could do well in the air force. The Civil Air Patrol staff and the air force staff had made a meaningful investment in us, and we all appreciated their efforts. I believed it would pay off for them in the long run.

I may have had a more painful trip than many of the cadets, but I felt I had gained a lot. I had met one of God's beautiful children, I had learned a lot about the air force and its mission and capabilities, and last but not least, I had boxed in a real boxing ring and not been downed by a member of the US Air Force.

I thanked the Lord for His protection on the trip and my time with Della. I looked forward to getting home, seeing my family, and working on my projects.

Civil Air Patrol cadet, a.k.a. Cadet Rocky

CHAPTER 32

Progress

Pepére caulked his fishing boat every spring with a sticky, string-like material. He used a putty knife and sometimes a screwdriver and small hammer to insert this material between the boards on the hull of the boat.

When he finished caulking, he and a friend would slide the boat down the railroad tracks into the saltwater. As soon as the wood hull hit the water, it started to swell. At first the boat always leaked. The small sump pump under the flooring had a float attached to the on-and-off switch. When the water rose in the boat, the float rose and turned the pump on to keep the leaking water under control.

The *Popular Mechanics* magazine made no reference to caulking the boat that I wanted to build. And neither did the plans display or describe a sump pump. How did they plan to keep the boat from leaking? That was a question I'd have to figure out later. Dad had commented that any boat without caulking wouldn't even float. Time would tell.

The hull of my boat was to be created by running long, thin strips of oak the length of the boat. The strips, or chines, needed to be thirteen feet long by two inches wide. They were to come together at the front of the boat to make the bow. The oak keel would be tied to the transom in the stern of the boat. Each oak strip needed to be treated with steam or very hot water so that it would bow and make the front of the boat attractive and practical. The front needed to be this shape in order for the bow to cut through the water smoothly at slow speeds. At fast speeds, the boat was designed to take up only two to three inches of water. A metal fin on the hull, or bottom of the boat, would keep it stabilized on turns. The garage was the perfect place to build my dream boat, but it had no access to steam or even hot water.

I really didn't want to build the boat frame in the basement because it had a dirt floor and a tendency to flood when it rained or when the snow melted quickly. The basement sump pump was supposed to keep it drained, but it didn't always work. But the basement boiler did have copper tubing circling the inside wall of the boiler. When the water in the copper tubing was hot, it was pumped into a storage tank. The water was untouchably hot, and my bet was that it would be hot enough to allow me to bend the oak strips. There was also a faucet off the tank, so I had convenient access.

With this in mind, I phoned the lumberyard in Sanford, Maine and placed the order. I told my dad I was ready whenever he was. I had saved some money but not enough to pay for the complete order. Dad had told me that he'd pay for the boat materials in return for the work I'd done in splitting and storing the elm firewood. He never said he couldn't or wouldn't. I didn't want to hurt his feelings or get him upset, so I didn't ask. But I hoped he remembered what we had agreed to and would cover the complete order.

Dad called Uncle Ted and made arrangements to borrow his car and trailer the following Saturday. I was so eager—Saturday couldn't come soon enough. On Saturday, we walked down to Uncle Ted's after lunch, picked up the car and trailer, and headed for Sanford. I took my detailed patterns with me just in case. It was a quiet trip. Dad and I didn't usually do much small talk. As I look back, I'm sure that wasn't a good thing.

Dad helped me select the best pieces of mahogany and oak and also a thick piece of waterproof plywood for the stern of the boat. Once this piece of plywood was braced by some mahogany, the outboard motor would be mounted on it. We hadn't planned this, but he also helped me select an assortment of brass screws to hold everything together. I enjoyed having him take the lead with the lumberyard personnel. He paid the bill with cash and just smiled at me. That smile made my day!

We had used up some of the elm firewood in the basement, so now there was room enough to build the boat frame there. The thin oak strips were to be reinforced with wider oak boards on the floor of the boat. Sheets of waterproof plywood would eventually be screwed and glued to those wider boards to finish the hull.

There were lots of snowstorms that winter, which meant I had a lot of shoveling jobs to do. That was good because I'd spent everything I'd earned. I had purchased an electric drill, a router, and three different hand saws. The drill was for the hundreds of screw holes I would make and countersink, and the router was for shaping the boat trim. The really good news was that I didn't have to buy a table saw because Dad had one. I found out later that the router wasn't needed because I could buy the oak trim at the local lumberyard. The router was one of my biggest investments that winter. Live and learn, so they say.

After gluing and screwing the four oak strips to the transom and the two vertical frames, I wrapped scalding hot rags around the bow end of the strips and bent each one with pipe wrenches. With C-clamps holding them together, I glued and screwed them tightly. This process took me hours. It was quite late when I finally finished. I cleaned up and crashed for the night.

During the night, I was awakened by the sound of someone walking down the cellar stairs, but I was too tired to care. I was comfortable and warm under the quilts and went right back to sleep. I woke up late the next morning. When I walked into the dining room, Dad was at the table eating breakfast. I looked at the clock and saw that it was after ten o'clock. I grabbed some cereal and fruit juice and joined him.

He started the conversation by asking how the frame was coming along. I shared that I had stayed up late trying to properly shape the bow and hadn't seen it since. Dad continued eating and so did I. He then said, "I suggest you check the kind of glue you are using."

"I'll do that," was my response.

He was not a subtle person; but at times, like Mom, he was very kind. I knew now what the noise on the stairs was last night, and I also suspected that there was a serious problem. I didn't go downstairs right away to examine the boat. I needed a few moments to collect myself and get ready for the bad news. After washing and dressing, I went down and took a look.

The glue hadn't held. I could move every joint with my hands. I quietly said to myself what was on my mind and headed up the cellar stairs. Downcast, I turned off the lights at the top of the stairs, walked into the kitchen, and ate two pieces of apple pie.

Dad walked by and asked, "That bad, huh?"

I looked up but couldn't smile. Eventually, I grabbed my coat and hat, slipped on my boots, and headed down the driveway. It was a beautiful day. The sky seemed unusually blue. The snow on the road and trees was melting, and I detected the scent of pine needles.

After walking for a half mile, I thought, *God has been so good to me in spite of the fact that I'm impatient and so stupid at times. He loves me as I am. He always forgives me and often before I forgive myself.* I prayed and walked until I got it out of my system. Then I headed back home—the sun seemed brighter and warmer on the way back. I unzipped the front of my coat and decided to enjoy the rest of the afternoon walk. Sometimes you just have to let go and give it to God.

Uplifted, I resolved to research and find the right glue and start over, but not today. I sat down in the den armchair. My brother climbed up on my lap and carefully slapped my cheek and I returned the slap. We started wrestling and laughing.

A week later, with the advice of experienced people at the hardware store, I purchased the right glue and larger brass screws. The joints on the boat now held as tight as steel. I also learned that Weldwood glue wasn't just for bonding; it was for making the boat watertight. I appreciated the expert advice!

Two weeks later, the oak frame was all glued and screwed together. I spent the following week sanding the frame. Some of the joints needed more glue, so I added some and then sanded again. This was as far as I could go on the boat until I raised more money.

It was time to take the frame out of the dirt basement and move it to the garage. The basement was too damp to work in, and spring was coming with all of its rain and the possibility of water in the basement. Julie seemed to know what was going on in the house all of the time, and most of the time we were friends. She mentioned that some people didn't believe I was going to be able to take the framed boat out of the basement through the bulkhead. In fact, the same people were betting the frame was too big and would never leave the basement. I thanked her, and she gave me that I-told-you-so smile.

I wondered who would do that. I was relying on Dad's help to carry it out. It needed to be tipped on its side and slowly slid up the steps and out through the door. I double checked my measurements and knew it was going to be tight. I was certain that whoever had bet against me had also checked the measurements.

It could have been Pepére for he was a betting man, but most likely it was Dad. I couldn't see my mom betting against any of her kids. Maybe it was Grandpa—nope, he didn't care about boats. It's got to be Dad for he is very detailed. I hoped I was wrong.

I was blessed with a strong mother. She loved work and, like her mother, never stopped. If she stopped working, she was napping. I asked her if she'd have the time to help me move the boat frame from the basement into the garage.

She smiled and said, "Sure."

She knew what was going on. We set a time to do it. Then she suggested that I might want to take the bulkhead door off before we started. She was a smart woman and I truly loved her. Without her encouraging me to go to Sunday school and church, I believe I'd never have come to know Christ as my Savior.

The oak frame with its heavy plywood and mahogany was almost impossible for the two of us to lift. We each wore gloves to protect our hands from getting oak splinters. With Mom at the bow and me at the stern, we tipped it on its side and dragged and pushed it a few inches at a time. It was a slow process. When we got it to the bulkhead stairs, I asked her to focus more on balancing the boat and guiding it through the bulkhead.

We found that lifting it through doorway was easier than pushing it across the basement floor. I had a good grip on the hull. With Mom's help, I slowly lifted it up the bulkhead stairway. Little by little it moved through the doorway with very little space to spare. Once it was balanced on the doorsill and the frame, we rested. I ran through the cellar and up the stairs and outdoors. Facing each other, we lifted it through the doorway and set it down on the snow. We were both sweating even though it was freezing cold. After catching our breath, we slid it across the snow and into the garage through the double doors.

I said loudly, "Somebody lost some money today!" and we both laughed.

I loved to see her happy. She was such a quiet person, but when she laughed you couldn't help but feel good inside.

CHAPTER 33

Skipper Ready

The boat frame lay upside down on the wooden garage floor. The oak and mahogany wood had been sanded clean and was ready to be covered with waterproof plywood. There was plenty of space in the garage to accommodate the boat and provide all of the room I needed to work on it. With enough space, good music, privacy, and a meaningful project, what more could a fourteen-year-old boy want?

To prevent the frame from moving when I was working on it, I boxed it by elevating it on some large wooden blocks and then tacked the blocks to the wood floor. I cut patterns for each of the pieces of plywood needed to enclose the hull. Paper shopping bags and tape patterns had worked for the boat frame, so why change? Besides, they were cheap.

The plywood was not as expensive as the oak and mahogany had been, and the store agreed to deliver. What a deal! There was plenty of snow shoveling and part-time housecleaning work around, so when I had saved the funds, I placed the order.

I had purchased three different wood hand saws before I started building the boat: a jig saw with lots of blades, a medium crosscut saw, and a fine finishing saw. They each came in handy for cutting the plywood. It didn't take long to learn that projects can go from fun to miserable based on the quality of the tools you have to use.

The *Popular Mechanics* magazine plans didn't come with instructions on how to build the boat or seal the hull. Therefore, I perceived my first challenge was to cut each plywood piece so that it would butt perfectly to the adjacent piece.

Unlike Pepére's big boat where the seams needed space to expand when wet in order to seal the hull, the joints of my boat should have no space to expand. Had I ever seen a boat like that? No, but I believed that if the joints were glued and screwed tight, leakage would be minimal. But time would tell.

I traced each pattern on the sheets of plywood before I started. Most plywood has one finished side and a poorer side. I paid a premium for excellent plywood and purchased only the sheets that were needed. I cut out one piece at a time and screwed and glued it to the boat before I cut the next piece. I intentionally cut the second and subsequent pieces a little larger than needed in case they didn't butt together exactly. These could always be cut and sanded again, but I couldn't afford to buy more plywood.

The glue set up pretty quickly, so I spot drilled holes for the brass screws and then spread the glue and clamped each sheet in position. Then I worked quickly to finish drilling and tightening the screws before the glue set. Each piece of the hull was its own miniproject, and I wasn't in a hurry to make a mistake, especially with Weldwood glue and hundreds of brass screws.

Two weeks later, the hull was completely formed. It was beautiful! Upside down it looked very large. Pepére helped me turn it over. We blocked it up using some of the same blocks plus grain bags to protect the hull. He was pleased.

He said, "You know, the trailer that I used for my speedboat is still out back. I'm not using it, so if you want to use it you can." I thanked him and told him I really appreciated that.

I was really concerned about the boat leaking and spent a lot of time inside the boat carefully applying glue to the seams between the boat frame and the plywood. When the glue dried, it was clear. Since I planned to varnish the inside of the boat anyway, I figured that the extra glue wouldn't hurt. That was the only way I could hedge my bet.

First I covered the front deck frame and narrow side deck frame with plywood. I trimmed the outside deck edge with oak trim and, as usual, glued and screwed it down. I sanded everything that wasn't soft to the touch until it was. It was coming along. Pepére was visiting more often. Dad and Pepére spent some time on the weekends sitting in the garage with their smokes and sharing stories. I noticed that they never turned the music on and wondered why.

I installed the front mahogany seat and the mahogany steering wheel holder behind the front seat, and covered the front and rear floors with plywood. Then I washed all of the wood clean and let it dry. I varnished every part of the boat, except the outside hull, three times and rubbed each coat down. We flipped the boat over and I painted the hull with two coats of white paint and installed the aluminum fin. Except for the steering wheel, brass lights, motor, and gas tank, the boat was finished, and I loved its look but, of course, was still concerned about the possibility of it leaking. And I had no idea where I'd get the money to buy those remaining items needed to make it run.

I thanked the Lord many times during the project for all of my blessings. I knew that everything good came from Him, so I didn't say much about the boat to the kids at school. I saw it as a gift and kept it private within my family except for sharing it with two neighborhood friends one day after school.

—⁂—

It was late spring and I was mowing lawns and helping customers with spring cleaning. I was able to purchase and install the brass handles the boat needed plus the steering wheel. The biggest challenge ahead would be the selection and acquisition of the outboard motor and accessories.

I applied for a bus boy's position at the Rochester Hotel on Portland Street. After filling out their application, the manager showed me around and explained what my duties would be. He and I got along just fine. Most of their customers checked in after three in the afternoon. I figured that I could be there about that time. It seemed like a great fit. The manager told me I had to bring him a work permit because of my age. He asked me if I knew how and where to get one, and I told him I did. We shook hands and I biked home in seventh heaven.

My folks were fine with the position, and I dreamed all night about the people I'd meet and the tips I'd earn. It wasn't a fancy hotel, but I wasn't a fancy guy; so it was perfect. I wondered if I'd have to wear a uniform, but figured I'd deal with that after getting the permit. I couldn't wait until morning. I biked to school and waited an eternity for the last bell, and then I was on my bike headed for the superintendent of school's office to meet my mom.

We waited in the reception area. I saw him through the open door and realized his son was in my sister's class. He was a nice-looking guy and about the size of Grandpa—large. The receptionist asked me to fill out an application. I printed everything neatly and signed it. She told me it would be a few minutes and headed into his office and closed the door.

We could hear his loud voice through the wall and closed door. After a while, she opened the door and motioned for me to come to her desk. She said, "I'm sorry. Your application has been turned down." When I pushed a little, she said, "That is all I can tell you. It has been turned down."

Neither Mom nor I liked to be told no. I knocked on his door and asked if I could speak to him. He said, "Come in," and directed me to have a seat. I explained to him that I needed a job and this one seemed perfect. His response was that it wasn't a job for someone my age. He was sorry but he had to do what was right.

I looked at him closely and saw his dark blue suit and neat tie. I saw his degrees in picture frames behind his desk and wondered what he knew about the hotel that I didn't know. I was upset and didn't want to leave. I tried to think of something to say that would change his mind but decided not to beg.

I didn't get mad right off—that wasn't my style. Some people can get mad and then get over it quickly. My style required that I didn't get mad but instead spend the next two weeks thinking about how to get even. As I biked home, I realized that it was hard to be a good Christian with my kind of style. I knew God had other plans, but I really wanted to experience the excitement of working in a hotel.

On the following Sunday, two things happened that took me by surprise: our septic tank overflowed for the first time that spring, and a church friend of Grammy's who worked at J. C. Penney's informed me that there was a stock boy's position open at the store and encouraged me to apply.

I applied for the position, got the permit, and started the following Monday. Why was I surprised? God loves me and when He closes one door, He opens another one.

We had cleaned out the septic tank many times, and Dad said it had a lot to do with our growing family. He'd had enough, and it was time to have a new leach field dug. I started asking questions about the field.

He asked, "What's on your mind, Jacob?"

"We talk about keeping money in the family, so why can't I dig the leach field? Just pay me a fraction of what you'd pay someone else and we both win." He didn't say anything. I waited.

Hesitantly, he replied, "Let me think about it." Later he agreed to my proposal.

It is interesting how different the layers of soil are as you dig below four feet of New Hampshire soil. The good news was that there was no ledge. I started the leach field ten feet away from the cement septic tank, just in case it overflowed again. I also bucketed some of the liquid and stuff out of the septic tank and hauled it down to the stone wall in a large garbage can in the wheelbarrow. I was careful, wore gloves, and bathed after I finished each time.

The leach field project took two weeks. I ran lights from the garage, so I was able to work on it late into the evenings. It basically was a six-inch fiber pipeline with holes in it running seventy to eighty feet and draining into a fifty-five-gallon drum. The drum and ditch were both filled with rocks. The more rocks the better the drainage. We had plenty of rocks on the stone wall and the wheelbarrow worked fine to haul them.

Pepére came up and sat in a lawn chair with his thermos and straw hat and made sure I wasn't lonely. Mom told me that he'd bring some of his friends up and take them into the garage when I wasn't around. That was good news. It was good to have his friendship and company.

The last part of the project was cutting a new hole in the cement septic tank and setting the cast-iron elbow and drain pipe correctly so that the tank would properly drain. Dad and I did that part together, and he sealed the cement around the pipe on the outside.

I could only work so long with the pick and shovel. It was hard work and tiring. Every day I worked on the project as much as I could and hoped it wouldn't rain hard until after it was finished.

Part of the leach field project deal was that Dad and Pepére would find a used motor for the boat and, if any repairs were needed on the motor, Dad would take care of them. I thought it was a good deal for both of us. Pepére was a tough trader, and Dad was no slouch.

They found a used Mercury outboard motor, and Pepére made sure it had enough power to make the boat fly. They tested it in a water tank before Dad purchased it. It was on the boat when I arrived home after work one day. I stayed up and waited for Dad to get home from work that night to thank him. We went to the garage and enjoyed the new motor together.

I installed the gas tank, which came with the motor, under the front deck and out of the way, and ran the feed line under the floor back to the motor. Then I installed the new hand throttle I'd purchased so that I wouldn't have to reach back to the motor.

We registered the boat and trailer. We were now about ready. Will it float or sink? No one was betting.

It was June and the sun was getting warmer. School was almost over and all I could think about was work and going to the lake and taking a ride on *Skipper*.

CHAPTER 34

The Mount

How does one describe Lake Winnipesaukee? Located at the foothills of the White Mountains, it is the largest and most beautiful lake in New Hampshire. Nothing in New Hampshire lives clearer in my mind than that lake. It quietly dominates everything around it. It is the center of attraction year-round. Even when it is covered with ice, it has much to offer those fortunate enough to live nearby. We lived about eighteen miles from its southern point, Alton Bay, but to me it was always just up the road.

Aunt Silvia, my mom's older sister, and her husband, Uncle Broderick, owned a summer cottage at a campground on Back Bay in Alton Bay. Uncle Broderick and his family usually spent two full weeks of summer vacation plus weekends at the lake. Their daughter Elsa loved being at the lake. My uncle worked as an electrical engineer in a suburb of Boston more than ninety miles away. They had a much longer drive to and from the lake than we did. We just drove up Route 11 eighteen miles, headed up the west side of the lake less than a mile, and turned left into the campgrounds.

In mid-June they invited us to spend the day there with them. During the visit, Dad mentioned that I had built a boat. Uncle Broderick asked where I was keeping it and Dad told him "at home for now." He laughed and kiddingly suggested we keep it under his cottage. Loving the idea, I quickly responded that I thought it was a great idea and, if he wanted to, he could use it. Astonished, he said, "Really, you would let me use your boat?"

Dad kidded, "We don't know if it even floats yet!"

Their cottage was built on the side of a hill that sloped to the bay. There was lots of storage space under the cabin, so after supper we agreed to bring the boat up the next weekend.

During the next week, I built a large cushion for my knees and installed it in the rear cockpit. A Class B racing boat can carry the driver in the rear plus two passengers seated comfortably in the front. The driver kneels in the rear with the front half of his feet in the two stirrups, resembling cutouts, in the rear floor. This kneeling position helps the driver balance the boat in rough waves and also allows him to lean forward over the steering wheel to help bring the bow of the boat down quickly in a racing start. All of this is done comfortably with the right hand on the steering wheel and the left hand on the throttle.

My sisters and brother were excited about going to the lake. With *Skipper* tied down and in tow, we all climbed into Pepére's car early Saturday morning and headed to the lake. Pepére also loaned me the canvas cover he'd previously used on his speedboat. Uncle Broderick and his family were driving up from Massachusetts and anticipated arriving around lunchtime. We planned to spend the rest of the day together.

The boat slid easily off the trailer and into the Back Bay water. We floated the boat close to shore with the motor tilted up. After I slipped on and tightened my life jacket, I climbed into *Skipper*. I'd been in her so many times before but not on water. She felt comfortable and her finish glimmered in the sunlight.

Dad suggested that I stay in Alton Bay on my first run. I experienced chills up and down my spine as Pepére and Dad slowly pushed me off. I looked down and all around the bottom of the boat; it was dry! I silently exclaimed, "Thank You, Lord." I tipped the motor back to its normal position and choked it. It started right up, but it was really loud. I waved and slowly headed down Back Bay and through the Route 11-B underpass and out into Alton Bay.

My whole family walked up to Route 11-B and crossed it to the grass on the other side overlooking Alton Bay. They were waiting for me to put *Skipper* through her paces. I didn't know why, but I was a little embarrassed. I squeezed the throttle a bit and she sputtered just once and then took off. I hung on a little tighter to the steering wheel and squeezed the throttle a little more, and *Skipper* lifted out of the water. I was amazed and exhilarated. She was flying. It was midmorning with no breeze, and the bay was smooth as glass. I headed back to where the family was watching and rode by them a couple of times.

The sides of the boat did not go straight down to the bottom of the hull. Instead, at eighteen inches down they angled forty-five degrees for a foot before they connected to the hull. This angle was called "nontrip chine." This design was supposed to stop the boat from flipping on sharp turns. The aluminum fin on the hull and the "nontrip chine" needed testing. I opened the throttle and turned sharply. The boat didn't even slow down. *Skipper* banked into the high-speed turn like an airplane does. I was impressed!

Now I needed to share her with the family. I headed for shore at the bottom of the hill where they were standing. I slowed down and turned the motor off and tipped it out of the water to coast to shore. There were a lot of rocks near shore, so I was very careful. I waved for my dad to join me. I floated to a large boulder, grabbed it, and pulled *Skipper* around so that Dad could climb in.

As I watched him walk down the hill and light a cigarette, I remembered his skeptical comment to Uncle Broderick: "We don't know if it even floats yet." I thought he deserved a little payback.

We cruised at half speed around the bay in the calm water and then headed north to open water. As we made the turn around the bend, we saw the *Mount Washington*, a huge scenic cruiser, heading straight for us about a quarter mile ahead. Based on the size of her wake, she was cruising close to full speed.

I squeezed the throttle a little and watched Dad's right arm point for us to cruise closer to shore. Slowly my mind was thinking through an alternative plan of action. I turned a few degrees toward shore to acknowledge Dad's signal. Then I squeezed the throttle and moved *Skipper* to three-quarter speed. She loved this speed and hummed to acknowledge it. The water was rougher now that we were out of Alton Bay, but *Skipper* rode the top of the waves and made little *bump, bump, bump* sounds. *Skipper* was ready for some excitement, and I was ready for a little payback.

I quickly turned her straight for the *Mount Washington*'s bow and squeezed the throttle wide open. The engine was humming at a high pitch.

The *Mount* blew her horn several times. I'm sure the captain didn't do it for us, but it was nice to think that he did. We didn't have a horn, but I planned to fix that.

About a hundred yards in front of her, I turned to the right and headed down her port side. We weren't dangerously close, but people were running to the rail to see what was going on. Just before we passed her stern, I pulled *Skipper* to port to cross the *Mount's* wake. We hit the first wave as it was curling up and it lifted us up and we flew into the air across the sudsy, churning wake. *Skipper's* engine screamed. As we plunged into the second wave, water came over the bow and, for a second, I wondered if we'd continue going down into the lake. But then the engine grabbed the water, and we shot up into the air and banged over a few more big waves until we were in the clear. It was thrilling—like a roller-coaster ride.

I finally looked at my dad in front of me. He was holding on to the front deck for dear life. The cigarette in his mouth was broken in half and the lit half was just hanging there. He and I were soaking wet and there was a lot of water in the boat. He was saying something, but all I heard was, "Take me to shore, take me to shore!"

It wasn't a voice of fear. It was the other sound that said, "do it now, Jacob, or else" sound. Now you understand my weakness. I knew that it would have been much smarter to get mad and get over it than to get even. I also knew that I was going to pay big this time.

I headed *Skipper* back toward the underpass and noticed the family was no longer on the side of the hill. We cruised slowly into Back Bay. Dad turned and said, "I will never ride in this boat with you again, and you are not to take your younger brother for a ride either!"

As he finished his last word, we noticed that Uncle Broderick and his family had arrived early and the entire clan was headed down to the water's edge to meet us. They were waving and Dad's arm slowly came up and waved. I turned the motor off and tipped it forward as we coasted close to shore. I heard Uncle Broderick ask Dad how he got so wet. Did he fall out of the boat? Everyone laughed as Mom handed Dad her towel. Their arrival may have saved my life!

We had a great lunch together and took turns sitting in the boat while my mother took pictures. We kids spent the early afternoon swimming in Back Bay while the adults hung around the cottage relaxing.

When it quieted down in the late afternoon, I took *Skipper* out for a long run. After stopping at the refueling station and refilling the gas tank, I cruised back to where we'd met the *Mount* and then headed further out into the broads. The huge lake was beautiful from every point of view. The hills and mountains surrounding it seemed so much larger viewed from *Skipper*. I wanted to cruise around Rattlesnake Island but needed to be back for supper, so I turned around and headed back to Alton Bay.

As I headed back to the cottage, I thought about how the desire to build a boat began. It was Pepére who had gotten me started by taking me fishing and letting me steer his boat. Dad and Mom had encouraged me by making suggestions when they saw me headed in the wrong direction and then helped finance *Skipper* by letting me take on projects that perhaps others could have done better. I considered myself truly blessed. What a day! I knew I'd never forget it.

After supper, Uncle Broderick took me aside and asked if I'd like to stay the night. He wanted me to teach him how to handle and take care of the boat. I told him I needed some clothes, and after he cleared it with Dad, we agreed that he'd follow us home and I could pick up whatever I needed.

We spent part of the next day going to church and Sunday school on the campgrounds. In the afternoon, Uncle Broderick and I took a ride on *Skipper*. I started out driving the boat, and then we switched when we got out into Alton Bay. He did fine. He didn't drive the boat very fast, which was okay.

When we got back, we lifted the motor off *Skipper* and hung it on a two-by-four-foot rack on the basement wall. Evidently, a motor had been hung there before. When I built *Skipper*, I installed large chrome-plated handles on the transom and the bow. Uncle Broderick and I lifted the boat out of the water and set it on some carpet-covered, wooden workhorses. We washed *Skipper* down and covered her with Pepére's canvas cover.

He asked me a lot of questions about how I had built the boat and shaped the bow and stuff like that. I thought, *Engineers sure are inquisitive people*. We had a friendly supper together with the rest of the family, and after evening church he took me home.

When we picked *Skipper* up at the end of Uncle Broderick's vacation, he had installed lights and a horn on the boat, plus purchased an oar and two nice life jackets for her. I thanked him for his gifts and he said, "No, thank you for sharing your boat with us."

It was good to know that sometimes one good deed deserves another.

CHAPTER 35

Mind Bender

Skipper was resting on Pepére's boat trailer and protected from the sun by his canvas. You couldn't see her impatience because she was hidden by the garage, but I knew in my heart that she, like me, was just waiting for another run on the lake.

I loved the fifteen-hour-long summer days. The heat of the early morning sun energized me. I could earn money all day long and after supper spend three more hours doing what I loved to do.

Biking back and forth to work was easy, considering I had waited a long time for a permanent part-time job. I was now the stock boy at our local J. C. Penney store. The store was clean. I did my share of cleaning and most of the other employees kept their sales space clean. The clothes were inexpensive and functional. The style was up-to-date but not ahead of its time. In the basement of the store was a small tailoring area and storage area. My basic work area was in the basement where incoming deliveries were inventoried, sorted, and made ready for upstairs display. There was just something about the store that made me feel it was one of America's best.

The women and men working there were always dressed neatly. It was nice to see the men wearing ironed slacks and shirts with ties every day. The ladies always wore stylish and colorful dresses. I never heard anyone talk about a formal dress code, but you could feel that there were unwritten standards. As stock boy, I was exempt from the white shirt and tie but had to wear slacks and a neat shirt, plus polished shoes. I used my first paycheck to buy work clothes. I thought that the clothes would look great when school started. Therefore, it was a two-for-one investment.

The store manager, Mr. Bender, was married with no children. He was a little formal at times but was always focused on serving customers. He didn't stay in his upstairs office. Instead, he was usually on the move encouraging staff to do this and that and warmly greeting customers by name. I watched him closely and thought highly of his style as a manager. It appeared to me that he put his customers first, his employees second, and himself last. It seemed like a profitable formula.

He asked me one day if I was still working part-time mowing lawns and weeding gardens. I remembered some of my prior experiences had been on my application. I told him I was doing it on a limited basis now that I was working at the store. He then asked if I would be interested in helping him clean up the flower beds around his home.

I was complimented and responded, "Of course I would." We set a time for the following Saturday morning.

Saturday came and I was up early. I did my chores, had breakfast, and biked to his home off North Main Street. His wife answered the door and walked me around the gardens and explained what she wanted done. She shared that Mr. Bender had to go to work, so she'd be working with me.

I got the wheelbarrow and tools out of the garage and started weeding the flower beds. She offered me a drink and I thanked her. She said she had to change into some work clothes. I watched as she headed for the back door. She had a rhythmic walk. I wondered what it was about older women that attracted me.

The gardens looked dry from summer heat. They were filled with beautiful flowering plants, but you couldn't see their beauty because of the tall weeds and dead flower stems. I filled the wheelbarrow and dumped the yard trash into one of three fifty-five-gallon drums behind their garage.

I was heading back toward the gardens with the wheelbarrow when Mrs. Bender came out of the back door with a tall glass of orange juice in hand. We met at the side flower garden. The juice was great, but I had a hard time swallowing it. She was dressed in a very low-cut blouse. It was like a bathing suit top with matching shorts. I had never seen such large busts in such a small top. I tried not to look at her as I finished my drink.

It was hard to focus on the area I was weeding. I kept thinking crazy thoughts and wondered why Mr. Bender had led me to believe I would be helping him, specifically. After finally getting past that thought, I wondered if this was some kind of a test. Finally, I stopped thinking and emptied the wheelbarrow again. It was hard work not looking at her. I thought about my first-grade teacher and what had attracted me, and I compared her to Mrs. Bender. They were completely different but still both ladies. The morning passed and she walked over and asked if I was ready to eat. I told her I was always ready.

She went into the house and I continued to work until she called. I washed my hands under the outside faucet as she set our lunchs on a small table under the maple tree. The French bread sandwiches were full of tomatoes, onions, and tuna fish. They were tasty and filling. I focused on the food but noticed she had put on a light sleeveless outer top. I thought, *Classy lady, good cook, and she dresses to highlight her strengths.* She was sociable and, I would have to say, very attractive. I thought to myself, *Mr. Bender appears blessed.*

We worked until midafternoon and the gardens looked attractive with their beautiful flowers clear of all the weeds and trash. There were actually many different gardens: one on each side of the house, two smaller gardens on each side of the front porch steps, and the backyard gardens.

I felt she was obviously pleased with the work because she paid me well for my time. She also asked if I'd be available again if she needed me. I said "anytime" and thanked her, but for some reason I wasn't in a hurry to leave. However, she turned like a classy lady should, said "bye," and closed the back door. I slowly biked home.

Obviously, I was overwhelmed by Mrs. Bender and wondered if she knew it. She had done all the right things. Was that a measure of a mature woman? I had never before felt as intense around a mature woman. I felt seriously guilty for my thoughts and needed help. I prayed on my way home that God would reset my thoughts—this had been a heavy-duty day.

Once home, I fed and watered the chickens and cleaned up for supper. Saturday night's supper was always beans and hot dogs. Not my favorite supper, but we ate it together as a family. After supper, I felt at peace and fully forgiven. I had learned a lot that day and decided to upgrade my image of an ideal future wife. She'd be a combination of the compassion, beauty, and charisma of my first-grade teacher, Miss Lemoore, and the classy style and sensuousness of Mrs. Bender. I figured that even God would find her acceptable.

With all of that heaviness and guilt behind me, I thought of *Skipper* as I fell off to sleep. How was I going to get her and me to Lake Winnipesaukee before I turned fifteen in July or before summer's end?

Maiden voyage

CHAPTER 36

Summer's End

Pepére was involved in fishing the Atlantic Ocean and wasn't around town much that summer. He had an apartment upstairs over a Main Street jewelry store, which was just down the street from where I worked. As I biked by his apartment on my way to work, I'd look up. If the window was open, I knew he was somewhere nearby. On those days, I often visited him during my lunch break.

Some days he hung out with his buddies on the corner—that is, until it got too warm. I loved to hear his buddies call him Henri. He dressed nicely, but no matter how hot it was he always wore long pants. He and my dad had that in common. They never showed their skinny, white legs in public.

Much of the time he and his buddies spoke in French. But when I arrived, he stopped whatever he was doing and grabbed me. He wasn't grabbing me to hug me; instead, he was trying to put me in a headlock. We weren't interested in hugging other guys. It just wasn't our style.

As we visited during one lunch break, I wanted to bring up the subject of taking *Skipper* to the lake but didn't know how to approach it. I didn't have a place to keep her even if I got her there and didn't have a plan to get her or me back home. In addition, I didn't have a place to stay at the lake; so I just spent time visiting with Pepére. I knew if the Lord wanted me to spend time on the lake with *Skipper* it would happen. So I waited. Waiting on the Lord had always been one of my biggest challenges, but I was slowly learning.

We covered a number of subjects and I needed to get back to work. As I turned to walk away he asked, "When are you going to take the boat out again?"

Surprised, yet happy that he asked, I simply responded, "I don't know."

"If you need a lift, just let me know."

He and God amazed me. I gratefully responded, "Thanks, I'll let you know." To myself I thought, *Thank You Lord, You truly know the desires of my heart.*

Once back to work, I tried to focus on other priorities. I kept thinking about the fact that I had a limited number of friends at the lake, which meant limited options. I only knew and had invested time in five people there: my uncle, aunt, and three cousins. If I wanted more opportunities to spend time on the lake, I figured I needed to find a way to invest in more potential friends there. It was either that or move there. I knew in my heart I was going to move away from home sometime in the near future, but I wasn't ready to even think about that yet. I really wanted at least one more summer of some fun with *Skipper.*

Summer was passing and my options were running out. I was saving money and upgrading my wardrobe with employee store discounts and specials. I shared the discounts and specials with Mom and my sisters and brother. She was able to buy a few special back-to-school items for my sisters and something for my brother.

One day, Elsa and her brother surprised me by visiting me at work. They said they were up for a few days and wanted to see where I worked. Elsa was sixteen but not driving yet. They mentioned that their parents were down the street looking for some bedding for their cottage. I got permission to leave for a half hour and went to see them.

They were just about finished shopping and said they were going to Grammy's for supper. I asked if they were planning to visit my mom. They looked at each other and then said they would come up after supper and visit for a while. It was good to see them and to know that they would make Mom's day when they visited.

I biked home after work and Mom was already making some dessert for them. "Good news travels fast," she said, as I walked through the kitchen.

The house smelled wonderful as the apple pies baked. She was such a good cook. I don't recall her ever making one pie. It was always two or more. Her motto was "Don't heat up the stove for just one thing." She had spread a special tablecloth on the dining room table and set out small dessert dishes and her delicate cups for coffee and tea. She didn't have many nice things but what she did have she enjoyed sharing.

They arrived that evening at seven-thirty. Mom started the coffee and heated water for tea. We met them at the back door and we kids headed outside to visit. Elsa had a lot to say, and Julie and I were all ears.

During dessert, Uncle Broderick asked me how the boat was running. I shared that it had been in a deep sleep since he had used it earlier in the summer. I thanked him again for all the stuff he had purchased and installed on it.

Aunt Silvia asked my mom if we'd be able to visit them at their cottage over the weekend. Mom thanked her for the invite and said she'd talk with Dad when he got home and let them know in the morning. Uncle Broderick added, "Jacob, bring your boat if you want to!"

I looked at Mom. She changed the subject. *She is so quick,* I thought.

After they left, Julie and I helped clean up. My job was washing the dishes, and Julie's job was drying and putting them back in the cupboards. For some reason, she always had to go to the bathroom during this time. Jackie and Monty were only six and four years old, respectively, so Mom and I finished up. I don't know what plumbing problem Julie had or what she did in the bathroom, but she sure took a long time.

Mom mentioned the conversation and told me not to get my hopes up for the weekend. I knew she and Dad would have a talk and it would be almost impossible to go to the lake without a car. I felt Mom missed out on too much by being stuck at home without transportation. Times were changing and Dad wasn't. She was getting impatient for more freedom and seriously wanted to go to work in one of the mills. She'd heard that there were jobs available in the spinning room, and she longed for the opportunity to interview for one of the positions.

She was such a hard worker, and I was sure things weren't going to stay the same forever. Dad was tough, but she was driven. I slept upstairs for many reasons, but I could still hear their conversations after he got home—and they were getting louder. One wanted no change; the other wanted a chance to improve the family's standard of living. I loved them both, but the level of conflict was escalating.

The morning came early. While Dad was still in bed sleeping, Mom shared with us kids our new plans for the weekend. Pepére had agreed to drive us up to the lake Saturday morning with *Skipper* in tow. We wouldn't leave though until Dad had had a good night's sleep and we'd all eaten a good breakfast.

Mom cautioned me, "Jacob, don't push him!"

Grammy and Grandpa would come up to the lake later in the day and drive us all back home after supper and games. We all cheered. I looked at Mom; she wasn't smiling. I wondered what price she had paid for our weekend fun.

Life was so complicated and stressful without transportation, but it didn't seem to bother Dad. Amazing! I had decided that before I turned sixteen I'd have wheels. I was tired of bumming rides off others. I never said a word to Mom, but soon I'd devise a plan to buy myself a car. Cash and wheels smelled like freedom to me.

Traveling to the lake again was peaceful. I thought about how little I knew about the rest of the world outside of New Hampshire. I spent a lot of time in both the public and the high school libraries but researching was not like actually traveling there, meeting other people, and learning about new opportunities. On the way to the lake, Pepére mentioned that he'd been inquiring about places on the lake to keep his boat because he was interested in fishing freshwater next summer.

It was good to be back in Alton Bay. We arrived at Back Bay and Pepére backed the trailer with *Skipper* on it into the water. I tied her up behind the cottage. Pepére stayed and visited for a while and then headed home. Before he left, however, he told me to let him know when I needed his limo to bring the boat home. I laughed and thanked him again and told him he was too good to me.

We spent the morning swimming in Back Bay and watching the *Mount Washington* take on passengers in Alton Bay. Elsa loved to dive for coins that were tossed into the water by the *Mount's* passengers. She didn't get much money but seemed excited by the danger of diving, especially when the boat's motors were running. I didn't think the risk was worth the small amount of change she got, but, as they say, to each his own.

Dad took *Skipper* out for a cruise. It brought back the memory of what he had said to me not so long ago: "Kids don't build boats!" When he returned, he took my brother and each of my sisters for a ride, and Mom took more pictures. Although he'd refused my offer to build him a boat, I got the next best thing—watching him enjoy mine. Dad kept his word about never riding with me again in *Skipper*.

After lunch, the girls headed to the roller-skating rink across from the entrance to Back Bay. I got to take *Skipper* out alone. I cruised down Back Bay and under the overpass into Alton Bay. I headed down the bay and refilled the gas tank with mixed fuel. The marina was busy with lots of noisy folks having fun.

I cruised out onto the bay and headed north to open water. It was nice to have lights and a horn on the boat and extra life jackets in case anyone wanted a ride. As I headed to the open water, I noticed a boat stopped and a young guy working on the engine. Keeping at a distance, I drove slowly around the boat; he waved for me to come closer. I pulled up and shut down the engine and used my new oar to paddle the remaining distance. He hollered, "I'm out of gas!" I threw him a line and we both tied it down, and *Skipper* proceeded to pull him slowly down the straights and into the bay. Eventually, we passed under the overpass and coasted into the marina.

He didn't have any money. I loaned him enough to half fill his tank so that he could get home. He asked me to follow him so that he could repay me. I stayed a little ways back as I followed him home. He pulled up alongside a beautiful boathouse and tied up his boat. I shut *Skipper* down and coasted into the shallow beach with my motor tipped forward out of the water to protect the propeller.

There were a lot of people sunbathing on the front deck of the boathouse, and some teenagers were in the water swimming. I climbed out of *Skipper* and sat on the shallow lake bottom preventing *Skipper* from getting any closer to shore. Soon Shane, the fellow I loaned the money to, and the teenagers helped me tie *Skipper* safely to the dock. They introduced themselves and invited me to meet their sunbathing grandparents.

Shane and Lonnie Cains were cousins and were spending part of their summer at the lake with their grandparents. Shane repaid the money and his grandfather thanked me for my kindness. Lonnie was tanned and shy—and she had a great smile. They were both my age and were impressed that I had built *Skipper*.

Shane worked in their family-owned garage after school and on weekends and today ran out of gas in his grandfather's old boat. They walked me through the boathouse where a huge inboard speedboat was docked. The boathouse was like a home on the water. It had a small kitchen, stove, refrigerator, and a bathroom. I was envious. I could live in their boathouse and think I was in heaven.

We swam for a while and I met some of their friends who'd come up for the weekend and were staying overnight. They walked me across the street and showed me their grandparents' cottage. The teenagers all slept on the large screened-in porch on convertible couches. The entire place was beautiful.

After that, we sat in the kitchen, drank some root beer, and talked about our families and the schools we attended. Shane was really focused on working in the garage when he finished school, and Lonnie just listened quietly. Every time I looked at her, she dropped her eyes. Interesting!

We exchanged names, addresses, and phone numbers, just in case we wanted to get in touch with each other. I shared that I enjoyed writing, but Shane said he wasn't much of a writer. Lonnie suggested softly, "Write to me, and I'll share your letters with Shane." Shane explained that they lived in the same neighborhood in Salisbury, Massachusetts and invited me to visit sometime.

It was time for me to go. I promised to look them up if and when I returned to the lake. *Skipper* started up nicely after I floated out to deeper water. We all waved good-bye.

I had some time left. I headed out to the broads and cruised along the beautiful shoreline. The water was clean and crystal clear, and the sun's rays pierced the light-blue lake water making it glisten and sparkle. There were a few boats around but not many. The late-afternoon breeze created whitecaps on the open broads, so I continued to stay near shore. I felt so blessed riding in *Skipper*. It was such a gift and I thanked the Lord many times for her and for all He had done for me.

The cruise back was too short, but I was high as a kite having made two new friends. I knew I'd see them again on the lake. With that in mind, I headed to the cottage and looked forward to fun with the family.

Grandpa was standing on the shoreline in his long pants and casual shirt. I pulled the engine out of the water and floated near the shoreline.

"Looks good!" he remarked.

"Get in. I'll take you for a ride," I replied.

He loved the water and could swim in the lake and ocean for hours at a time. Cold water never bothered him for some reason. I took him for a ride out in the bay and down the shoreline. He sat there comfortably with his hair blowing in the wind. I cooled it and didn't go very fast as I wasn't sure how he'd enjoy getting wet.

When we returned home, Mom was waiting on the back porch of the cottage with her camera in hand and came down to take our picture. Grandpa thanked me for the ride and headed to the front of the cottage where the guys were playing horseshoes.

After tying *Skipper* to the shallow dock and washing her down, I quietly climbed up the cellar stairs and peeked into the kitchen where Grammy and the women were starting to get things ready for supper.

Mom gave me a hug and said, "You sure are getting tan, Jacob."

The girls were working on a huge puzzle in the family room, and Monty was busy with some toys he'd found in one of the upstairs bedrooms. I joined the men who were sitting out front in lawn chairs. Uncle Broderick said they had played horseshoes for two hours in the sun and needed to rest. He asked me how the ride went. I responded that the lake was smooth as usual. I then shared that I'd met two kids across the bay that were my age and had spent some time with them. Dad was smoking his cigarette. He didn't talk much around Grandpa.

Uncle Broderick mentioned that he and Dad had discussed leaving my boat there for a couple of days if it was okay with me.

"That's fine with me. I've got to talk with Pepére about picking it up anyway."

Uncle Broderick continued by saying that he was going to have a trailer hitch and appropriate wiring for tail and brake lights installed on his car. Therefore, he could drop it off on his way home Monday night.

I was about ready to thank him again when he said, "I'm not just doing this for you. I'm planning to build a boat for myself soon and this will be my first investment in that project."

Aunt Silvia stuck her head out the door and told us that supper was almost ready. Boating was forgotten in a second. I thought, *It must be in the blood, because food sure got everyone's attention.*

The pressure was off. I could trust Uncle Broderick with *Skipper*; I was sure he'd use her to do some fishing on Sunday and Monday. He was the first person I thought of as an intellectual in our family. Being an electrical engineer for the Public Service Company, he'd done very well for himself. He was always reading the newspaper, and his cottage and home contained stacks of periodicals and shelves loaded with books of all kinds. It wasn't just him though, it was also Aunt Silvia. They both shared the love of books. Aunt Silvia hadn't graduated from college as he had, but we all knew that in time she would. She wasn't the kind of person to play second fiddle or be left behind.

Supper was great as always. The laughter around the table focused on the kids and their attempt at roller skating. Uncle Broderick told a lot of jokes and it was wonderful to watch Grammy laugh as tears filled her eyes.

The ladies quickly cleaned up the dishes so that there would be time for games. I slipped into the front room and grabbed some of their newspapers and periodicals and headed upstairs where Monty was playing on the floor with some toys.

—⁂—

Earlier in the year our first nuclear submarine, the USS *Nautilus*, was launched in Groton, Connecticut. I made a model of a World War II submarine and kept it on my brother's toy shelf at home. I was thinking about competing in next year's school science fair, and nuclear fission was something that interested me.

Not long after the *Nautilus* was launched, the US Air Command deployed the B-52 Stratofortress. I enjoyed the Civil Air Patrol and looked forward to seeing the B-52 up close. There was a chance that Portsmouth would be named a Strategic Air Command base, and I hoped that our unit could visit it.

The most important news was about the Salk polio vaccine. In early spring it had been introduced in mass quantities and was proven 80 to 90 percent successful. One of my cousins had polio and everyone was scared to death their children would contract it.

—⁂—

When I arrived home from work on Tuesday, there was a letter on my desk from Lonnie. I thought, *She must have written and mailed the letter Saturday or Sunday for it to arrive so quickly.* She wrote as she talked, softly and quietly. Lonnie said "they" were this and "they" were that, and I thought, *It wasn't "they" anything. Shane was a guy's guy and he wasn't anywhere around when she wrote this letter.* I could still see her smile and tanned skin. I could also see the beautiful boathouse and cottage. Their lake property was like a dream place to me.

We wrote two or three times a week. Then, one Saturday, Dad handed me three letters and asked, "What did you do to that girl?"

I said, "I didn't do anything, we're just friends."

He disbelievingly responded, "Sure!"

I sometimes thought that what he said to me told me more about him than it did about me. I couldn't read his mind, but I knew he was sending me a signal. With him working nights, it really prevented us from developing much of a trust relationship. It seemed to me that we all pay a price when we don't invest enough in each other—or maybe I was just paranoid.

—⁂—

As the end of summer approached, Elsa invited Julie and me up to the cottage to attend a special Christian teen event at the Back Bay campground. We happily went. I also saw it as a possible opportunity to

215

see Shane and Lonnie again. After church on Sunday, I asked and got permission to visit them.

Shane, Lonnie, her girlfriend, and I went to a movie in a small theater on the bay. There weren't more than twenty people attending the afternoon movie, and I don't remember what was playing. I do remember sitting next to Lonnie, between Shane and Lonnie's friend. This was new territory and we said nothing to each other during the whole movie. I was frozen in my chair; the tension was unbelievable, but I wouldn't have traded seats with anybody.

Shane told some jokes to help us all relax. We laughed too loud and eventually left the theater before the movie ended. It was better than being told to leave. We stopped for ice cream cones and walked back to their cottage. Everyone was getting ready to close up for the season—it was a sad time at the lake when the season ended.

Skipper and I had a great run at the lake that summer, and I had a new pen pal. When puberty shows its face, I learned that a pen pal of the opposite sex can help take some of the pressure off. Lonnie was always a lady in correspondence and I tried to always be a gentleman, but just the fact that I had a sweet girl to share things and events with helped.

I was truly blessed. I had a sweet grandmother and mother in my life and now I had a sweet female correspondent. It was healthy for me and I hoped it was as healthy for her. Our friendship lasted until we each got engaged to someone else many years later.

Dad and Jackie in *Skipper*

CHAPTER 37

Timing

As a preteen-ager, I enjoyed being part of a team. Whether it was a scout organization, church group, or sports team it was good to be involved with others working towards a common goal. At the same time, those groups did things together that I could have never done with my family or on my own. The Boy Scouts raised money for two special ninety-mile trips to Boston where we attended a Boston Braves baseball game and a Boston Celtics game. These two trips raised my level of awareness and expectation.

As a high school student, I decided not to join as many organizations. I moved from a lot of team activities to more individualized priorities. The move wasn't intentional and it was very subtle. Maybe puberty drove the change or had something to do with my longer-term thinking and trying to prepare for the future. Either way, team identification was fading as a significant social need.

In my youth, I found that the most powerful encouragement came from finishing something I started. I didn't want to just finish it, but finish it well. In fact, if it wasn't excellent I derived no encouragement from the project at all. At the same time, almost every significant project I finished involved some assistance from others. Sometimes the people may not have realized how much they had contributed, but I knew how significant their roles had been. I don't believe I would have accomplished much without them. Whenever I found myself in trouble on a project, most likely it had something to do with my lack of listening to others or ignoring their advice.

Because I had rebuilt a bike, and built a bike trailer, a lamp, a desktop cabinet, a vanity, and a boat, I was confident I could build almost anything if I set my mind to it. I was gaining confidence in my planning ability and problem-solving skills as well, but I found that my biggest challenge was finding the funds to do something substantial.

The projects I had completed so far were driven by my basic needs and my desire to do something for my parents. The lamp and desktop cabinet completed my home study and bedroom needs, the vanity was for Mom, and the boat was to have been for Dad. The boat became mine by default. I enjoyed it and so did my dad; that was very important. He and Mom worked very hard to keep us fed, clothed, and healthy, so I truly wanted to bring them some joy.

Much of my satisfaction came from the utility of each finished project; for example, driving *Skipper* around the lake. The second-best feeling came from watching Dad and my brother, and sometimes my sisters, cruise around the lake together. My mother took pictures of Dad and my brother riding in *Skipper* and she gave me extra copies. That picture framed my finished project. Its purpose was to give Dad something special because he had no luxuries. Every time I looked at that picture, I experienced the feeling of accomplishment and the joy of giving.

Because I was only thirteen and fourteen when I built the boat, it had been a challenging project for me. The project was made easier because wood was forgiving. However, the next project was going to involve more metal and machine parts. I'd learned a little about working with metal when I built the bike trailer and the vanity. Metal required many different tools. Most of the tools in our garage were designed to be used for working with wood and doing simple repairs, not the rebuilding of a car.

Both Pepére and Grandpa owned cars. All of my uncles and aunts owned cars, but we still didn't. The lack of a car caused some contention in our home. Mom was a hard worker and was prepared to go to work to earn more money, but Dad had said no. I figured he had his reasons, so I never asked. They seldom argued in front of us, but in a small house you didn't need a stethoscope to hear what was going on.

The fact that we didn't have a car usually didn't bother me. Because I'd learned how to drive at a very young age while spending time working on family farms and staying with close relatives, driving a vehicle wasn't a big deal to me. I had my bike and the freedom to try and earn as much as I needed. I couldn't ask my parents for more.

—⁂—

The old 1926 Chevrolet tractor, the one I'd been run over by years earlier, was still sitting in tall grass in the back field looking as if it needed attention. I spent some time cleaning it up and painting it green and yellow. Then I built a floor on it and moved the gas tank, suspending it over the front hood. When my dad reviewed my work, he laughed and suggested I move the gas tank to a safer place, which I did. The tractor was fun to work on but too slow to run on the road. I guess I worked on it as an interim step before facing the challenge of rebuilding a car.

My income stream could not support the purchase of a fully-functional car—defined as one that would be safe on the road. I'd heard many people say that there is more than one way to skin a cat, which meant I had to find another way to acquire and/or build my future wheels. I figured that my alternative was to buy a junk and rebuild it. My reasoning was that since I had successfully built a boat from scratch, I couldn't see why I wouldn't be able to rebuild a car even though I didn't have any auto repair experience. (No emotion and pride there, right?)

I decided to start researching junks immediately and sought my dad's approval. He said, "No. This family can't afford a car, so how can you afford one? Until you are sixteen and have a regular job, forget it."

They say ignorance is bliss, so I continued to search for an old junk. I found a 1932 Ford Roadster for sale. It had already been chopped and channeled. It had a flathead Ford V-8 engine in it and was clean of rust. The doors, which were leaning against the trunk, were in fair shape. The front end was detached and except for the radiator grill lying beside the car with grass growing through it, the car didn't have much else.

I asked my dad again if I could buy a car. Again he said, "No, they are expensive. Do you know how much a new car costs today?"

My response was, "No."

He explained that "new Fords cost three thousand dollars; the average American worker earns one dollar and eighty-five cents an hour; fuel costs twenty-nine cents a gallon; and then there are insurance, registration, and maintenance costs. So put it out of your mind."

I wasn't really listening. I was hooked on my next project and didn't like hearing the word *no*. Somehow my young and immature mind blocked out what I had previously learned about honoring my parents and, specifically, the part about obeying them.

There were two brothers who lived up the street on a corner lot. Their farmhouse was very old and in dire need of repair and painting. There was junk on their porch and more scattered all around the property. The buildings were set back from the street about twenty-five yards and nearly hidden by the tall grass in their yard. However, under a large elm tree about fifty feet back from the farmhouse was a fairly new three-car garage or workshop. It was neat, clean, and out of place in their unkempt yard. The best part was that it didn't appear to be in use.

The two brothers never bothered anyone. There was one time, however, when the cops stopped their old truck and arrested one of them for drunk driving, but that was all of the bad news. The good news was they had an unused garage.

I really liked our garage and workshop and wanted to buy the Roadster and work on it there, but Dad had blocked that move. I was determined to try to rebuild a car and wanted to start it soon. Emotionally, I wanted to talk to him about the Roadster, but I knew he would get hot and the heat would blow in my direction. I had two choices: back off and don't do it, or move ahead and hope for the best. I wrestled with the decision to move forward knowing somewhere down deep in my soul that if I didn't obey my parents my project wouldn't have God's blessing.

With the decision made, I knocked on the brothers' farmhouse screen door. This little guy with a coal-black beard opened the door and stepped outside. We talked about his garage and I asked if he would rent me a stall. He asked me a few questions, and I explained to him I needed a place to store and work on a car for a little while. Then he asked how long I was interested in renting, and I suggested a minimum of three months. He responded with a dollar amount for three months' rent, paid in advance, which included free electricity. The deal was done and I paid him. I thought, *This is the first time I have indirectly bought somebody booze.*

It was exciting! I had the fifty dollars I needed to purchase the car; but it was the weekend, and I was being closely supervised. I'm sure I'd been pushing the freedom window, and Dad was tracking me closely.

Dad's work was off and on, which meant he was now home some evenings during the week. This was all new territory for me. Consequently, when I got home from odd jobs or after-school sports, I had to account to him for my time. He and Mom had trusted me all of the time he worked second shift, so why didn't he trust me now that he was home? I didn't get it.

I knew he had serious employment and cash-flow issues to deal with, so I played it cool and made an extra effort to keep my chores current and my nose clean. Not working seemed to make him unpredictable and sometimes much more emotional than usual. Dad kept busy part of the time working around the house, but he wasn't emotionally into it. He seemed to be caught up in the union/management issues at the woolen mill.

One evening he came home from the plant after having met with other union members about the issues they faced with management. He called me into the kitchen. A chair was in the middle of the room. Dad reviewed some things he felt I'd done wrong and said that my attitude needed adjusting. I leaned over the chair, taking the position. He gave me a taste of the strap twice.

He then said, "If you'll promise not to do it again we can end it here."

I replied, "Dad, I'd like to promise, but I know I'll do it again and then I'll receive twice as many for breaking a promise. So let's finish it!" He laughed and it was obvious he couldn't finish. He told me to go upstairs.

I know his intentions were good, but I had grown up with my afternoons and evenings free as long as my mother knew where I was and what time I'd be coming home. Dad, however, appeared to want a much tighter rope on me and wasn't pleased with my part-time jobs, or me working at all. I didn't know how to give them up. I was hooked on incoming cash and gaining my financial freedom; I didn't know how to live without them.

I loved my dad and knew he had a family leadership role to play, but I had developed the routine of planning and managing my own time during his absence and wasn't interested in being corralled. I knew this was serious, but I couldn't go back to being a kid hanging around the house, seen and not heard.

The weekend ended and the fifty dollars was burning a hole in my pocket. Monday came and Dad went back to work—thank heavens! I biked out to the auto shop. The Roadster was still sitting in the grass. I told the owner I wanted the car on the condition that they deliver it.

The car was delivered on time at seven o'clock on Wednesday evening. I had them back it into the rented garage and block up the front end so that I could work on it. They signed a bill of sale. I paid them the fifty dollars and then locked the door of the garage with my new Yale lock. I went home so excited I couldn't get to sleep until two o'clock in the morning.

The streetlight on the corner provided enough light for me to see the farmhouse and the roof of the garage where my new project was waiting for me. I sat at the window dreaming of how I'd rebuild my new 1932 Ford Roadster. I thanked the Lord for my new gift, hoping somehow I would receive His blessing.

I'd spent all of my cash, so it was back to work. It took a couple of months to save money for parts and tools so that I could begin working on the front end. When I started reading up on how to repair and rebuild cars, I began to realize how little I knew about automobiles. I spent some time in the auto shop at school asking questions, and everyone was helpful. People in the car repair business were gaining my serious respect.

I was also realizing I was truly alone on this project. I couldn't talk to Pepére about it, for he would share with Dad. I couldn't ask my dad any questions. I had set myself up and had no alternative but to go it alone. I was overcommitted and had lost a lot of objectivity. Not the signs of God's blessings.

One afternoon as I was lying flat on my back under the car working on the front end, I looked up and saw Dad standing there looking down at me. There was disappointment in his eyes. I slid out from under the car and knew this wasn't going to be fun.

He didn't blow up, but asked a lot of questions. I told him the whole story. I wanted to say I was sorry for disobeying him, but I really wasn't.

Dad told me he had to go to work and quietly encouraged me to not pay anymore rent for the space and to bring the car home and put it in our garage. Then, with his lunch bucket in hand, he turned around and walked down the street headed for his ride. I felt terrible!

I had been able to put the front end back together, so all I needed was someone to help me push it down the street and into our garage. Two of my classmates came over later in the week and helped me move it. I was out of money again, so it sat there untouched for a couple of weeks. It was soaking up every dime I was earning.

I felt Dad wouldn't wait much longer to talk with me about the next steps. I wondered what the punishment would be. He was very strong and physical. He had put me on the ground a few times for being out-of-line, so I never knew when he might use his strength to straighten me out. Whippings with a strap were one thing, and I could handle those, but the physical stuff was starting to create deep resentment in me.

It was time. We were both sitting in the den in opposite lounge chairs. He said he needed to make me aware of something he was thinking about doing. He mentioned reform school and said that he'd been considering sending me there. His research showed that all he had to do was sign a document and I would be gone. My first thought was that it was pretty cold-blooded, considering that I'd never committed a felony or even a misdemeanor. On second thought, if he believed I was out of control, maybe he had some justification. He had said many times that in his house and under his roof I would do exactly what he said or else. Looking forward, I could see my life was going to change shortly. It wasn't really a surprise. I'd been pushing the freedom window for a long time.

Three passages from Scripture kept coming to mind:

1. Honor thy father and thy mother: that thy days may be long upon the land which the LORD thy God giveth thee (Exodus 20:12).

2. Children, obey your parents in the Lord: for this is right (Ephesians 6:1).

3. Honor thy father and mother; which is the first commandment with promise (Ephesians 6:2).

I had honored them in every project except for the Roadster. The car was all about me and not about my parents or my family. I knew in my soul that things had changed and would never be the same again. My dad had told me, the Bible had told me, and now there was a price to pay. I could no longer live here, and I had to prepare to move on—hopefully not on foot. Either way, I was not going to reform school.

Neither of my parents said anything about my garage rental and the Roadster purchase. I knew where Dad's head was and assumed Mom's position was I'd bitten off more than I could chew. She was willing to let time teach me a lesson. We were still on speaking terms, but I wasn't sure how much longer I was going to live at home—my choice or Dad's.

The good news was that Dad was back working full-time, fishing with Pepére on Saturdays, and I wasn't in reform school yet—but I'd been warned.

The more I researched what had to be done to rebuild the Roadster, the more I realized I was in way over my head. I didn't earn a dollar eighty-five per hour and had invested nearly one hundred dollars in a potentially beautiful classic car. There were not enough hours in the week and not enough part-time jobs to fund my rebuilding project. It was time to bring it to an end. I had to trade the Roadster for a vehicle requiring much less work.

I played it cool, stuck close to home except for part-time work and school, and lost myself in books about successful people who had started without anything. Time passed, and I felt there was breathing room. I had a bill of sale, so I started planning the next step. I had spent some money on tools and repairing the Roadster—in fact, just enough to get the front end working. I read all of the papers and stayed close to the school shop guys and believed in time I'd find a functional car and someone who'd take the car in trade.

There were many groups of people in our high school bound by a common bond. There were Future Farmers of America guys and girls, auto shops guys, jocks, cheerleaders, class officers, intellectuals, band members, actors, performers, smokers, and many more. I solicited everyone I knew, no matter what group they associated with, hoping they might help me sell or trade the Roadster for finer wheels.

I thought about putting an ad in the paper just to sell the car but decided not to because I felt a trade up would be a better deal for me. Slowly I was building a pool of cash from part-time work and felt it was only a matter of time before something would pop. Then it happened! One of the car guys at school told me there was a 1940 Ford Coupe for sale on a dealer's lot for one hundred and twenty-five dollars, and they would take a trade plus cash. I biked to their lot, introduced myself, and described my Roadster. They were interested.

They stopped by the house the next afternoon and looked at the Roadster. The owner and his buddy were impressed and said they would do the deal if I had seventy-five dollars in cash. It didn't take me long to find a ball point pen, some paper, and the seventy-five dollars. They wheeled the car onto their trailer, handed me two sets of keys, and parked the Ford Coupe in the driveway in front of the garage. They took their dealer plates off the Coupe and wished me luck.

They say money talks and everything else walks, and I believed it. I drove the car around the back lot and then parked it on the other side of the house. It was late Friday afternoon and no one was home; so I figured out of sight, out of mind.

—⁂—

It was a surprising weekend. It began early Saturday morning with my dad up and dressed for company or travel. He was sitting at the breakfast table when I came downstairs. I filled my plate with a couple of pancakes and some sausage and joined the family.

Dad asked, "Traded one for another?"

"Yes, I did," I responded.

"Does it run?"

"Yes, it does."

He pulled three one-hundred-dollar bills out of his pocket and laid them on the table. I asked him if I could touch them, and he let me. I had never touched a one-hundred-dollar bill before. He shared that he and Mom had decided to buy a car, and Pepére was picking him up at ten o'clock to take him to finalize the purchase. He shared that the three hundred dollars paid for the car in full and that he'd be back for lunch and then take us all for a ride.

Finally, Dad had taken the plunge and invested in a new life. I knew in my heart that mom's whole world would change, and mostly for the better. Our family finally had joined the rest of the new world. We were no longer country bumpkins—we had wheels.

That afternoon was filled with riding in the country and then washing the car when we got home. Sunday was easy; no waiting for a ride. We just got in the car, drove to church, and then parked it in a safe no-bump-or-scratch zone.

Mom was glowing. I loved it. Whoever said timing wasn't everything didn't get it. When my father made the decision to invest in a car, the entire family's focus changed, and from that moment on cars were something to be treasured.

I was more pleased with my father's new car and the flexibility it gave the family than I was with my project. I still biked back and forth to school and saved my money to purchase insurance and register the car when I got my driver's license. I didn't mind waiting. I just didn't know how much time I had.

Dad's car was too big for the garage; so he was fine with me keeping my Ford in it. (The car continued to be called "Jacob's work-in-process.") I could clean it, wax it, and work on it all I wanted to while listening to music in my clubhouse. I thought the car was beautiful. Its classic shiny, black finish, chrome hubcaps, and dual exhausts made it all I'd ever dreamed of as a car and it actually started—most of the time.

What more could a fifteen-year-old boy want than the freedom to try and live his dreams? I was content but remembered what Dad had said about reform school, and I knew the end of my contentment probably wasn't far off. He was not a man to threaten without the will to follow through. I believed the only reason I was still home was because my mom had not signed off on the deal. Here is another fact of life I was learning: sometimes when you accomplish your personal objectives, you lose.

Grandpa and Jacob in *Skipper*

CHAPTER 38

Fifteen

A year before, playing freshman football had added a new dimension to my life: namely, the opportunity to excel at something violently physical, but this time with social approval. It had been an introductory year with a lot learned about the rules and basic dos and don'ts. We were assigned positions based on our speed and our ability to catch or not catch the football.

Very few players on the team were standouts. Those who physically matured faster than others seemed to succeed, and those who matured at a slower pace didn't hit or run as hard. I differed very little from the others except for my speed and desire to tackle. I had no interest in carrying the football; blocking for others and chasing down and tackling someone were the things I loved to do. I never intentionally hurt anyone—it was the hitting and the chase that excited me most.

During that freshman season, our high school football coach asked two of us to practice with the high school team. We believed he asked us as freshman to join the varsity team because we ran faster than the other players on our team.

It was now late August. I was a sophomore and we were in the middle of summer football training. It was hot and practice was tough, but not as tough on me as on many others because I was already in pretty good shape as a result of all the physical labor and biking I'd done. However, after practice each day, three of us linebackers ran the track just to develop more stamina. I was now focused on learning the skills of playing football. The teamwork part was easy, having been a member of many other organizations. The toughest challenge for many of us included not only listening and learning all of the plays but getting the timing down just right.

Most of the guys on our team weren't physically large, but we were fast and loved to hit. I ended up playing the positions of offensive tackle and defensive linebacker. That year we went undefeated in our division. The keys had been our coaching, speed, coordination, stamina, and desire.

My sophomore English class was taught by a teacher who had lost her fiancé in World War II and never married. She was intelligent and very sensitive. One day she commented, "Behind every successful man is a great woman."

It crossed my mind that this appeared to be another one of her unsupported general statements. I asked, "What is behind all of the men that fail, including drunks and bums?" I was thinking about my neighbor who had shot himself and about my grandmother's drunken brother.

My teacher immediately told me to leave the classroom and go to the principal's office. I sat in his waiting area until the class was over and then the three of us met. She convinced the principal that I had intended to embarrass her, and she wanted me tossed out of school. I respected her English teaching skills but not her general conclusions about life. The principal listened to her and asked me for rebuttal. I told him I thought her general statement was unsupported and needed to be challenged.

I was instructed to go home and not come back without a parent. On my way home, I thought about the situation and concluded that she overreacted emotionally, and I was wrong to have rebuffed her general statement. I guess she just got under my skin that day.

I'd been in this boat before but was much less comfortable this time with the thoughts of reform school in the back of my mind. I was giving my dad justification—if he needed any—to sign the papers. This was not my intention for I was not ready to leave home yet.

The family car made it possible for Mom to drive me to school the next day and meet with the principal. He welcomed Mom and reminded her that he'd been my dad's football coach many years before. She listened but didn't appear to understand what I'd done wrong. The principal explained to her that he believed I knew better than to have challenged her statement. I'd made a wrong choice and that was enough reason for him to send me home. It seemed that knowing and doing the right thing was my biggest issue, especially when it came to keeping my mouth shut when I disagreed with an adult's opinion.

When returning to class, I kept my mouth shut and eventually earned a B in the class. I knew I didn't need any more episodes and neither did my parents.

—⁂—

It was almost impossible to earn much money during football season. Between practices and games there was little time left. I hated being broke. When the season ended and the snow arrived, I worked every spare minute I could. The difference was that we now had a family car, which meant that the driveway had to be cleared before I left the house to work other jobs. The only disappointing thing about relying on shoveling snow for income was that the weather had its own schedule. After school most of the snow had been cleared and only cleanup jobs were left.

I had quit working part-time at J. C. Penney's for football, and I missed the professional environment, the regular paycheck, and working with people who cared and focused their energies on serving customers. I had spoken to the manager, Mr. Bender, and asked if I could come back after football, but he had said, "No, I will look for someone who is sincerely interested in a longer-term relationship." I didn't want to get married; I just wanted to work and play football. It seemed to me that he made a bad decision for the both of us.

My odd jobs of cleaning windows, walls, and ceilings continued, but nothing was significant enough to raise the amount needed for car registration, insurance, and some repairs the Ford Coupe needed; therefore, it stayed parked in the garage.

I had a friend in my class, Mark Polinski, whose dad operated a small grading business and also owned some timberland on the road to Farmington. Mr. Polinski needed some trees cut down and limbed, and I suggested to him that Mark and I do it. With my dad's permission, I borrowed his two-man crosscut saw and ax. We planned to work at least two full days, Friday and Saturday. (Friday was teacher's day off.)

We took a cooler of food with us, a jug of water, tools, and some kerosene and oil to keep the saw slick. Mr. Polinski delivered us to the lot and gave us specific instructions on where and how to fell the trees. His plan was for us to provide the logs and he'd deliver them on one of his commercial trailers to the lumberyard. We'd get paid after the lumber was delivered.

At the end of the first day of work, I thought I'd never walk or bend over again. Every muscle in my back and stomach felt as if it had been torn from pulling that hand crosscut saw back and forth all day long. That evening I crashed before eight o'clock and crawled out of bed at six the next morning. Mr. Polinski was scheduled to pick me up at six-thirty. I was ready just in time. He had this habit of giving me "horse bites" on my leg. He did that by pinching some skin between his thumb and forefinger and then twisting it to make it hurt like a real horse bite does. He was amazingly strong, and with one hand gave me a knot that lasted thirty minutes. I tried to do it to him but couldn't even get a grip.

We got through day two and walked to the top of the hill around four o'clock and looked at our work. Logs were lying in all different directions, looking like dropped pick-up sticks on a rug. Nevertheless, I thought it looked pretty good. However, Mr. Polinski didn't agree. Disappointedly, he told us he'd have to use a bulldozer to lift the logs out of our mess and chewed us out all the way home. I wondered if he was just trying to get out of paying us our share.

Two weeks later, Mr. Polinski delivered me a check for my share and tried to give me another horse bite. The guy was nuts but honest. Still, it wasn't enough money to cover the cost of insurance, registration, and repairs. I began to think that rebuilding and owning cars wasn't in my best interest. In prior projects, things had always worked out, but not this time. I felt as if I was always behind with too little too late. My conclusion was that my project was not being blessed and may never be. Why should I be surprised?

On April 27th, Rocky Marciano, the undefeated Heavyweight Boxing Champion of the world, announced his retirement. I had watched many of his fights and loved how he planned his moves and never gave up; his tenacity and character made him one of my strongest role models. Unlike some successful professionals, he stepped up and served his country in the military. Not this year, but I knew that someday I'd serve just as he, Dad, and Pepére had.

—ɯ—

The school year was almost over, and I was up-to-date on all of my schoolwork. Summer was in sight. I stopped by the principal's office and asked if he had a few minutes to talk in private.

"Sure, come on in." He got up and closed the door. He wasn't aloof and knew what was really going on most of the time. My guess was that he'd seen it all. He sat down and then asked, "What's on your mind, Jacob?"

I took a seat across from his desk and told him I was leaving home to find work for the summer. I was current in all of my studies and had finished all of the class assignments for the year. My hope was to leave ahead of the crowd, considering there would be a lot fewer summer jobs available based on what I'd read in the newspapers. I asked him for permission to leave school a week early.

He asked me how my parents felt about my leaving and I shared as little as I had to, but enough to let him know I couldn't find full-time work anywhere in the area because of my age, so I was going to go where no one knew me. I also shared that things weren't good with Dad and me. He was considering sending me to reform school, and I wasn't interested in going. I told him that time needed to pass and two birds could be killed with one stone if I left for the summer. He promised to check with my teachers and get back to me—and he'd keep our conversation private.

I anxiously waited for two days before he called me into his office. He closed the door and tried to discourage me from leaving home. When he failed, he told me that each teacher had confirmed my work was done, and that he'd make sure my school records showed that I'd completed all of my courses.

He asked me to do one thing before I left and that was to have a talk with the football coach. I hadn't talked with anyone who'd had a conversation with the coach. Most said, "He talked and I listened," but I agreed to try. During my scheduled appointment with the coach, he surprised me by handing me some football shoes, a kicking tee, and a football. He asked me to practice kicking in my spare time and to be back there by August 24th for practice. I thanked him and looked for a bag for the stuff so that I could carry it home on my bike.

As I walked down the hall, I heard his loud voice ask, "You are coming back, right?"

I turned and replied, "I'll be here on August 24th, Coach."

My first thought was that he was worried about the equipment he loaned me not being returned, but then I thought better of myself. On the bike ride home, I was thankful that all was well with school. I prayed for a clean heart and the wisdom to complete my next steps carefully.

Thinking back to the biblical story of Abraham, I wondered what must have been on his mind as he prepared to follow the Lord's instructions: "Get thee out of thy country, and from thy kindred, and from thy father's house, unto a land that I will show thee" (Genesis 12:1). He was seventy-five years old when he left and must have truly trusted the Lord. I wanted to trust God just as much as Abraham had, and I also wanted His blessings.

I had enough money to register and make a deposit on car insurance, but I was only fifteen and wouldn't turn sixteen until July 22nd. It was late May and I couldn't drive for three months on just a learner's permit, especially out-of-state. The car was not a blessing—it was a burden. Again, I had disobeyed my father, so why should I be surprised?

It was Thursday night and all was quiet. Time was almost up. I knew that the heaviest amount of traffic on Friday afternoon would be headed north to the mountains with a lighter amount headed south to Boston. If I headed out of town instead of going to school in the morning, no one would be the wiser until later in the day. I believed that the principal would understand when I didn't show up at school, even though he'd still have to make the call to my home.

I didn't sleep much. I wrote a short note and left it on my bed for Mom to read. It explained that I was going to be on the road looking for summer work and not to worry. I promised to call often and would do my best to stay safe. I believed she knew it was time and that it would only get worse if I stayed. I also believed she couldn't hold my dad back much longer if he decided to send me to reform school. She'd done so much for me so often; I didn't want to cause her pain. By calling her frequently, I could mitigate some of the pain this would cause.

My plan was to come back for more clothes as soon as I had found a meaningful job, so packing my gym bag was easy. I packed light, taking a couple of shirts, an extra pair of pants, a few changes of socks and underwear, and a shaving kit bag with all of my dental and shaving stuff. As I planned on sleeping in the parks or the woods until I found work, I also took my light jacket and a woolen, long-sleeve shirt that Grammy had made me. It was lined in all of the right places. On the coldest days, I found it warmer than a sweater and not as bulky. With my maps, address book, small Bible, note pad, and a couple of pens stuck in the bag side pockets, I was about ready. I had less than fifty dollars but felt it should last me at least a week to ten days. I took a long look at the football stuff and decided to leave it behind for now. My first focus was on finding work, not practicing football.

My leaving was carefully planned; it wasn't emotional. I needed to get away and find meaningful work during the summer. I was determined to bring home three hundred dollars for car registration, insurance, and spending money during football season when I wasn't able to work part-time. I was strong and looked older than my age. It would be dangerous, but what's life about if it's not planning to accomplish something meaningful and then trying as hard as you can to achieve it?

I headed out earlier than usual that Friday morning and with some trepidation left the bike in the garage. I knew that my family would be praying for me. With Christ as my traveling companion, I walked briskly down Franklin Street headed for the foot of Rochester Hill. Once there, I stuck my thumb out for a ride south to the neighboring town of Dover. In just a few moments, I was on my way to begin my first summer on my own.

1940 Ford Coupe

Afterword

Jacob was not interested in what a normal fifteen-year-old teen was supposed to be happy doing during the summer months. He wanted to work and earn enough money to drive his 1940 Ford Coupe to school in the fall while playing high school football.

He was driven to find work in another town where no one knew his age. He knew the road would be dangerous but decided the rewards were worth the risks.

Jacob's true story continues in *Mentor's Glory*, which we hope to publish later. Watch for its publication on CrossBooks.com.

Music

Jacob grew up in a generation when music was part of everyday life. He loved all kinds of music, as it set the tone for whatever he wanted life to become. Background or in-your-face, it made life more enjoyable in the worst of times and sweeter in the best of times.

The following information was sourced from http://www.information fromanswers.com:

* 1947 (6 years old)
    o "He's Got the Whole World in His Hands" by Mahalia Jackson
    o "How High the Moon" by Ella Fitzgerald
    o "Blue Moon" by Bill Monroe and The Bluegrass Boys

* 1948 (7 years old)
    o "Tennessee Waltz" by Redd Stewart and Pee Wee King
    o "Country Boy" by Boudleaux and Felice Bryant
    o "It's a Most Unusual Day" by Jimmy McHugh and Harold Adamson
    o "Candy Kisses" by George Morgan
    o "Red Roses for a Blue Lady" by Sid Tepper and Roy Beaumont
    o "Buttons and Bows" by Jay Livingston and Ray Evans
    o "I'll Be Home for Christmas" by Patti Page, Kim Gannon, Walter Kent, and Buck Ram

- 1949 (8 years old)
  - "The Hokey Pokey" by Larry Laprise
  - "Melodie D'Amour" by Henri Salvador
  - "Dear Hearts and Gentle People" by Sammy Fain and Bob Hilliard
  - "Mona Lisa" by Jay Livingston and Ray Evans
  - "Rudolph the Red-Nosed Reindeer" by Johnny Marks and Robert May

- 1950 (9 years old)
  - "Music, Music, Music" by Stephen Weiss and Bernie Baum
  - "My Heart Cries for You" by Percy Faith and Carl Sigman
  - "Rag Mop" by Jonnie Lee Wills and Deacon Anderson
  - "Silver Bells" by Jay Livingston and Ray Evans
  - "Cherry Pink and Apple Blossom White" by Louiguy, Jacques Larme, and Mac David

- 1951 (10 years old)
  - "In The Cool, Cool, Cool of the Evening" by Hoagy Carmichael and Johnny Mercer
  - "Kisses Sweeter than Wine" by Huddy Ledbetter and The Weavers (Pete Seeger, Lee Hays, Fred Hellerman, and Norman Gilbert.)
  - "Unforgettable" by Irving Gordon
  - "Mockin' Bird Hill by Vaughn Horton and Patti Page
  - "I'm a Fool to Want You" by Frank Sinatra, Joel Herron, and Jack Wolf
  - "It's All in the Game" by Charles Gates Dawes and Carl Sigman
  - "Be My Love" by Nicholas Brodszky and Sammy Kahn
  - "Come on-a My House" by Ross Bagdasarian, William Saroyan, and Rosemary Clooney
  - "Cold, Cold Heart" Hank Williams

- "It's Beginning to Look a Lot like Christmas" by Meredith Willson

- 1952 (11 years old)
    - "Do Not Forsake Me" by Dmitri Tiomkin and Ned Washington
    - "Don't Let the Stars Get in Your Eyes" by Slim Willet
    - "Your Cheatin' Heart" by Hank Williams
    - "When I Fall in Love" by Albert Selden
    - "You Belong to Me" by Jo Stafford
    - "Botch-a-Me" by Rosemary Clooney
    - "Count Your Blessings (instead of Sheep)" by Irving Berlin

- 1953 (12 years old)
    - "I'm Walking behind You" by Billy Reid
    - "Ruby" by Heinz Roemheld and Mitchell Parish
    - "You, You, You" by Lotar Olias and Robert Mellin
    - "That's Amore" by Harry Warren and Jack Brooks
    - "C'est Si Bon" by Eartha Kitt
    - "Santa Baby" by Eartha Kitt
    - "White Christmas" by Bing Crosby and Rosemary Clooney

- 1954 (13 years old)
    - "Mr. Sandman" by Pat Ballard
    - "The Naughty Lady of Shady Lane" by Sid Tepper and Roy C. Bennett
    - "Cross over the Bridge" by Bennie Benjamin and George Weiss
    - "Sh-Boom" by James Keyes, Claude Feaster, Floyd F. McRae, and James Edwards of the Crew Cuts
    - "Shake, Rattle and Roll" by Charles Calhoun
    - "I'm Ready" by Muddy Waters
    - "That's All Right, Mama" by Arthur Crudup; recorded by Elvis Presley

- 1955 (14 years old)
  - o "Rock around the Clock" by Bill Haley
  - o "Maybellene" by Chuck Berry
  - o "Cry Me a River" by Arthur Hamilton; recorded by Julie London
  - o "Love and Marriage" by Jimmy Van Heusen and Sammy Cahn
  - o "16 Tons" by "Tennessee Ernie" Ford

Notes

Chapter 1

o   References to the Isinglass River: Wikipedia at http://en.wikipedia.org/wiki/Isinglass_River.

Chapter 2

o   References to the G.I. Bill of Rights: Information at Answers.com at http://www.answers.com/topic/1946.

o   References to President Truman: Information at Answers.com at http://www.answers.com/topic/1947.

Chapter 6

o   References to "The State of Israel Is Proclaimed": Information at Answers.com at http://www.answers.com/topic/1948.

Chapter 14

o   References to Rocky Marciano: Wikipedia at http://en.wikipedia.org/wiki/Rocky_Marciano.

Chapter 16

o   References to Piscataqua River: Wikipedia at http://en.wikipedia.org/wiki/Piscataqua_River.

o   References to Sarah Mildred Long Bridge: Wikipedia at http://en.wikipedia.org/wiki/Sarah_Mildred_Long_Bridge.

Chapter 18

o   References to Hercules bike: Wikipedia at http://en.wikipedia.org/wiki/Hercules_Cycle_and_Motor_Company.

Chapter 21

o   References to Edmund Hillary: Information at Answers.com at http://www.answers.com/topic/1953.

Chapter 22

o   References to General MacArthur: Information at Answers.com at http://www.answers.com/topic/1951.

Chapter 31

o   References to Loring Air Force Base: Wikipedia at http://en.wikipedia.org/wiki/Loring_Air_Force_Base.

Chapter 36

o   References to the USS *Nautilus*: Information at Answers.com at http://www.answers.com/topic/1955.

o   References to the B-52 Stratofortress: Information at Answers.com at http://www.answers.com/topic/1955.

o   References to Salk polio vaccine: Information at Answers.com at http://www.answers.com/topic/1955.

Dad and Monty in *Skipper*

B/25/P